IMAGES OF WAR

Early Jet Bombers
1944-1954

In the decades after the Second World War Britain, America and the Soviet Union all built fleets of jet bombers capable of carrying nuclear weapons. The graceful delta-winged Avro Vulcan was one of a trio of V-bombers which acted as the British nuclear deterrent in the 1950s and 1960s.

IMAGES OF WAR

Early Jet Bombers
1944-1954

RARE PHOTOGRAPHS FROM WARTIME ARCHIVES

LEO MARRIOTT

Pen & Sword
AVIATION

First published in Great Britain in 2019 by
Pen & Sword Aviation
an imprint of
Pen & Sword Books Ltd
Yorkshire – Philadelphia

ISBN 978 1 52675 389 2

A CIP catalogue record for this book is available from the British Library

Typeset in 12/14.5 Gill Sans by
Aura Technology and Software Services, India

Printed and bound in CPI UK

Pen & Sword Books Ltd incorporates the imprints of Pen & Sword Archaeology, Atlas, Aviation, Battleground, Discovery, Family History, History, Maritime, Military, Naval, Politics, Social History, Transport, True Crime, Claymore Press, Frontline Books, Praetorian Press, Seaforth Publishing and White Owl

For a complete list of Pen & Sword titles please contact

PEN & SWORD BOOKS LTD
47 Church Street, Barnsley, South Yorkshire, S70 2AS, England
E-mail: enquiries@pen-and-sword.co.uk
Website: www.pen-and-sword.co.uk

Or
PEN AND SWORD BOOKS
1950 Lawrence Rd, Havertown, PA 19083, USA
E-mail: Uspen-and-sword@casematepublishers.com
Website: www.penandswordbooks.com

Contents

Glossary

AFB	Air Force Base
AV-MF	Aviatsiya voyenno-morskogo flota (Soviet Naval Aviation)
CG	Centre of gravity
ECM	Electronic countermeasures
EW	Electronic warfare
ft	foot/feet. Unit(s) of Imperial measurement of distance
ft/min	feet per minute (relating to rate of climb)
GAZ	Soviet state aircraft factory
GE	General Electric
KG	Kampfgeschwader (Luftwaffe unit corresponding to an RAF Wing or USAAF Group)
kph	kilometres per hour
lb/lbs	pound(s). Unit of Imperial measurement of weight
lb.s.t.	Pounds static thrust (measure of the power output of a jet engine)
NAS	Naval Air Station
NATO	North Atlantic Treaty Organization
OCU	Operational Conversion Unit
OKB	Soviet design bureau
PVO	Protivovozdushnaya oborona strany (Soviet Air Defence Force)
PR	Photographic Reconnaissance
RAE	Royal Aircraft Establishment
RAF	Royal Air Force
RATOG	Rocket Assisted Take Off Gear
RN	Royal Navy
SAC	Strategic Air Command
SBAC	Society of British Aircraft Constructors
shp	shaft horsepower (measure of a turboprop's power output)
SNCASE	Société Nationale de Constructions Avions Sud-Est
SNCASO	Société Nationale de Constructions Avions Sud-Ouest
SNECMA	Société Nationale d'Etudes et de Construction de Moteurs d'Aviation
US	United States

USAAF	United States Army Air Force (1941–7)
USAF	United States Air Force (from 1947)
USN	United States Navy
VVS	Voyenno-Vozdushnye Sily (Soviet Air Force)

Credits and Acknowledgements

Unless otherwise credited, all the images in this book (except those in Chapter 5) are sourced from the Still Pictures Library of the US National Archive and Research Agency which is based at College Park, Maryland. In particular the invaluable assistance of Archive Specialist Holly Reed and her colleagues is very much appreciated.

Except where noted, all the images in Chapter 5 (USSR) are from the Russian Aircraft Research Trust, administered by Nigel Eastway, to whom grateful thanks for his assistance is due.

Images from other sources are denoted by the following abbreviations.

AB	Air Britain
AC	Author's Collection
APC	Aviation Photo Company
ASM	Air Sea Media copyright image
MoD	Ministry of Defence (Crown Copyright)
NARA	US National Archive and Research Agency
PG	Peter Gilchrist Collection
PRM	Peter March (PRM Aviation Collection)
RART	Russian Aircraft Research Trust
USAF	United States Air Force
WC	Wikipedia Commons

Introduction

By 1910 the aeroplane had advanced from being an interesting invention to become a machine with practical applications and military and naval forces around the world began to take an interest in this new dimension of warfare. Initially the aeroplane was seen as a useful reconnaissance tool, especially as two-seaters carrying an observer were introduced, but it was not long before more warlike capabilities were introduced. In 1911 the first bombing raid was carried out by an Italian pilot flying a Bleriot XI monoplane when he dropped four hand

The concept of strategic bombing was formed in the First World War with both sides using specially-designed bombers to attack targets away from the front-line fighting. German Gotha bombers began raiding targets on mainland Britain in May 1917 while British Handley Page O/100s and O/400s carried out increasingly heavier day and night raids over France and Germany from mid-1917 until the end of the war. An O/400 is here being loaded with 112lb bombs. AC

A twin-engined biplane capable carrying a 3,000lb bomb load, the American Martin NBS-1 was a typical bomber design of the 1920s. It was bombers of this type which controversially sank the ex-German battleship *Ostfriesland* during a demonstration exercise in July 1921. Their commander, Billy Mitchell, was famously court-martialled for this action which nevertheless demonstrated the growing potency of air power.

grenades on Turkish troops in Libya. Three years later the world was at war and the technical development of aeroplanes progressed in leaps and bounds. Light bombers on either side worked mostly in support of the ground battle but by 1918 the concept of attacks on strategic targets away from the front line by a new breed of heavy bombers was established. Between the wars considerable effort was put into the design and construction of bombers and for a while there seemed to be no practical way of preventing mass attacks of the kind demonstrated in 1937 by the German Condor Legion when it mounted a savage raid on the town of Guernica during the Spanish Civil War.

During the Second World War the fate of campaigns hinged almost entirely on the outcome of air battles. While the German Luftwaffe concentrated on tactical bombing in support of army operations, the Allies gradually built up their strategic bomber forces using a new breed of four-engined heavy bombers such as the B-17 Flying Fortress and the Avro Lancaster. By 1945 the latter was dropping massive 10-ton Grand Slam bombs but even these were eclipsed in the Pacific where high-flying B-29 Stratofortresses had already destroyed many Japanese cities using a

First of the RAF's four-engined 'heavies', the Short Stirling first flew in May 1939 and entered service with 7 Squadron in August 1940, in whose markings it is shown here. Although outclassed by the later Halifax and Lancaster, it remained in service with Bomber Command until September 1944.

The Boeing B-17 Flying Fortress provided the backbone of US bomber forces in all theatres during the Second World War (this is a B-17G of the 91st Bombardment Group based at Bassingbourne, England). After 1945, the B-17 and its stablemate, the Consolidated B-24 Liberator, were quickly phased out of service in favour of the new B-29 Superfortress.

combination of conventional and incendiary bombs. On 8 August 1945 Hiroshima was wiped off the map by a single atomic bomb and a second attack on Nagasaki a few days later brought the war to a close but ushered in an era when the bomber had become a weapon of mass destruction and the arbiter of any future conflict.

In the new atomic era the United States, Britain and Russia all gave high priority to the development of a new generation of jet bombers capable of carrying an atomic bomb over great distances. This was quite a challenge as at that time a single atomic bomb weighed not less than 10 tons, although eventually lighter versions became available which could be carried by smaller tactical bombers such as the Canberra. During the so-called Cold War the threat of attack by fleets of bombers carrying nuclear and thermonuclear weapons was enough to maintain an uneasy peace by acting as a deterrent. Throughout the 1950s and 1960s the bomber maintained that role but by the end of that period it was passing to land and sea-based long-range ballistic missiles carrying multiple nuclear warheads. Consequently, although there was still a need for tactical bombers, the heavy bomber was gradually phased out of service although a few such as the B-52 still perform a useful function with the ability to deliver substantial concentrations of high explosive (as demonstrated in Vietnam).

First flown in 1947, the Boeing B-47 Stratojet illustrates the great advance in bomber design achieved only two years after the end of the Second World War. Like many new combat aircraft of the period, it relied heavily on concepts pioneered by the German wartime engineers and designers.

Today, conventional bombing is generally carried out by multi-role aircraft such as the F-35 Lightning II, Typhoon or F/A-18 Hornet (any of which can carry a greater bomb load than any Second World War bomber) and the concept of a dedicated bomber aircraft is virtually extinct. A notable exception is the B-2 stealth bomber but this was only produced in small numbers and has a highly-specialized role.

This book explores the development of the first generation of jet bombers and includes those in service during the period 1944 to 1954 as well as others which at least flew in prototype form during that time, in which case their subsequent career is briefly outlined. However, it is interesting to note that relatively few other new bombers were subsequently developed as the role of the bomber changed and was absorbed by other categories of combat aircraft.

Chapter 1

Germany

From the time that the German Luftwaffe was officially created in 1936 its operational doctrine was almost entirely directed to the support of army operations. By the outbreak of war in 1939 it possessed a substantial force of tactical bombers such as the Junkers Ju 88, Dornier Do 17 and Heinkel He 111, not to mention the much-feared Ju 87 (Stuka) dive bomber, but no serious effort had been made to develop a strategic heavy bomber such as the contemporary British Short Stirling and the American Boeing B-17. Amazingly by 1945 the vast majority of German bombers in service were still only derivatives of those earlier types. The only significant attempt to develop a heavy bomber was the Heinkel He 177 which first flew in 1939 but was plagued with a series of problems, mostly related to its complex DB610 engines, and its operational career was very limited.

However, the German aircraft industry was quick to realize the potential of jet propulsion and ultimately was the only nation to produce an operational jet bomber

The Dornier Do 17 light bomber was originally designed as a high-speed transport and the prototype flew in 1934, its slim lines earning it the appellation 'Flying Pencil'. It was subsequently developed as a light bomber and entered Luftwaffe service in 1937 although it was withdrawn from front-line service by early 1942. However, development of the basic design resulted in the Do 215 and Do 217 which were both active until the end of the war in 1945. Shown here is the second prototype Do 17M in which the liquid-cooled inline engines of the earlier versions were replaced by air-cooled Bramo Fafner 323-A1 radial engines.

(the Arado Ar 234 described in this chapter) during the Second World War. Unlike the British jet engines based on Frank Whittle's work with centrifugal compressors, the German engineers opted from the start for axial-flow turbojets (the BMW 003 and Jumo 004) which potentially were more efficient. However, development was frustrated by various technical problem and a shortage of vital raw materials such as nickel and cobalt so that it was not until mid-1944 that engines suitable for operational use became available and it was around that time that the Allies began to encounter the Ar 234 jet bomber and its fighter stablemate the Messerschmitt Me 262. Fortunately, from the Allies' point of view, their heavy strategic bombing campaign so disrupted manufacturing and training facilities, fuel production and surface logistics that the numbers available for combat were severely restricted.

In addition to the development of jet engines, German designers and engineers made dramatic advances in the field of aerodynamics far in advance of anything on the Allied side. By the end of the war they had flown aircraft with swept wings, delta wings and even tailless designs such as the Horten/Gotha Go 229. Although the Ar 234 was relatively conventional in terms of its airframe, the revolutionary Ju 287 was flown in prototype form and featured an unusual swept-forward wing plan. On the drawing boards were even more advanced designs such as the Junkers EF130 flying wing, the Blohm and Voss P.188 with a W-shaped wing planform, and the tailless Horten XVIIIB, although none of these were actually under construction when the European war ended in May 1945.

A contemporary of the Dornier Do 17 was the Heinkel He 111, which first flew in 1935 and entered service towards the end of 1936 and was later deployed by the German Condor Legion during the Spanish Civil War. The basic design was continually updated and developed throughout the Second World War and some were still operational in April 1945. Both of these bombers illustrate the German policy of developing existing aircraft types rather than introducing new designs.

The only German heavy bomber to see operational service was the Heinkel He 177. Despite appearances, it was actually a four-engined bomber, the nacelles each containing a DB610 engine which was formed of two DB605 units driving a single propeller through a coupled gearbox. Theoretically a good idea, in practice it was a technical nightmare and the He 177 achieved little success as a strategic bomber although did better in the anti-shipping role when equipped with Hs 293 guided missiles. This is the fourth prototype (He 177 V4) which flew in 1940 but was lost shortly afterwards when it failed to pull out of a dive. AC

The world's first operational jet bomber was the Arado Ar 234 'Blitz' which entered service in September 1944, initially as a high-altitude reconnaissance aircraft. Development of this amazing aircraft began as early as 1940 and two prototypes were virtually complete by the end of 1941. Unfortunately the development of the Jumo 004 jet engine lagged considerably behind and it was not until 15 June 1943 that the Ar 234 V1 finally got airborne. The slim fuselage and high wing left little room for a retractable undercarriage so a trolley arrangement was adopted which was jettisoned after take-off, the aircraft using retractable skids for landing. AC

There were no less than seven twin-engined Ar 234A prototypes, all of which utilized the jettisonable trolley. However, it was quickly realized that such a system was unsuitable for operational purposes and the airframe was modified to allow the installation of a narrow-track tricycle undercarriage in which the main wheels retracted into the central fuselage while the nose wheel retracted into a bay below the pilot. This resulted in the standard production version, the Ar 234B.

The Ar 234's slim fuselage was entirely taken up with fuel tanks and the undercarriage bays, leaving no room for a bomb bay. Consequently any ordnance had to be carried on three external hardpoints, one under the fuselage centreline and one under each of the underwing engine nacelles. The latter could carry a 500kg (1,100lb) bomb or an auxiliary fuel tank, while the maximum-size bomb which could be carried on the centreline was the 1,400kg (3,086lb) PC1400. Various combinations were possible but the maximum total bomb load could not exceed 1,500kg (3,300lbs).

Although the Ar 234 was designed around the Jumo 004 turbojet, consideration was given to a four-engined version using the slightly less powerful but lighter BMW003 turbojet. First flown on 8 April 1944, the Ar 234 V6 was powered by four of the latter units housed in single underwing nacelles and, as with the other prototypes, it still utilized the trolley undercarriage. Production examples of the four-engined version were designated the Arado Ar 234C.

Above: The Messerschmitt Me 262 was perhaps the most outstanding combat aircraft produced by any nation during the Second World War. With swept wings, axial-flow jet engines, tricycle undercarriage and a heavy armament of four 30mm cannon, it was far in advance of anything else in service in 1944–5. Had it been available earlier and in greater numbers it could well have altered the course of the air war over Europe. The Me 262 V3 jet-powered prototype flew as early as July 1942 but combat-ready aircraft were not available until August 1944 and then only in small numbers. *AC*

Opposite below: The Ar 234 V8 and V13 (shown here) featured a revised installation of the four BMW003 engines in paired underwing nacelles and was fitted with a conventional undercarriage. In fact this prototype flew in February 1944, before the V6, and subsequent tests proved the superiority of this arrangement from an aerodynamic point of view which was adopted for all C-series variants. The four-engined variant offered a considerable improvement in performance and, although maximum bomb load remained the same, maximum speed (without external bomb load) at around 20,000ft rose from 461mph to 542mph and service ceiling from 32,800ft to 39,400ft. It was intended to produce the Ar 234C in several variants including reconnaissance, bomber, ground attack and night fighter and several prototypes were produced and flown but none reached operational units before the end of the war. *AC*

Above: In November 1943 Hitler attended a demonstration of the Me 262 and immediately decreed that it should be developed as a bomber. This seemingly bizarre idea is often held to be responsible for the delay in introducing the Me 262 into operational service but in fact this was entirely due to development issues with the Jumo 004 jet engines which were not overcome until early 1944 and despite Hitler's directive priority was initially accorded to the fighter version (Me 262A-1a). However, a bomber variant was eventually produced as the Me 262A-2a Sturmvogel (Stormbird) which could carry two 500kg bombs on racks under the centre fuselage as shown. *AC*

Opposite above: A captured Me 262-2a at the Luftwaffe test centre at Rechlin. The engine cover plates indicate that this is the Me 262 V7 prototype but that is unlikely as that aircraft was unarmed whereas this example has the standard nose-mounted 30mm MK 108 cannon. However, it is a bomber version as the two bomb-carrier pylons are visible below the nose and each of these could carry one of the 500kg (1,100lb) bombs visible in the foreground. The first operational bomber unit was KG 51 which received its first aircraft in July 1944 and subsequently participated in the Battle of the Bulge (December 1944) and Operation Bodenplatte (a major attack by massed Luftwaffe formations on Allied airfields on New Year's Day 1945). It continued operating until April 1945 when its bases were overrun by French and US forces. *AC*

Opposite below: The Sturmvogel was basically a dual-role fighter/bomber but a single prototype of a specialized bomber variant, the Me 262-2a/U2, was produced. This featured a revised forward fuselage with a glazed nose to accommodate a bomb aimer who was provided with a standard Lofte 7D bombsight. This entailed the deletion of the four 30mm cannon. The tactical purpose of this variant is not clear but it could possibly have acted as lead ship of a formation of single-seat Sturmvogels who would synchronize the release of their bombs with the actions of the leader. The sole prototype is shown here in a sorry state after being captured by US troops in May 1945.

Opposite above: A rare photo showing the captured Me 262A-2a/U2 being dismantled. Although of poor quality, it is of interest as it shows the forward hatch which allowed accesses to the rather cramped bomb aimer's compartment. *AC*

Opposite below: While the straight-winged Arado Ar 234 was a relatively conservative design, in 1943 a Junkers design team under Dipl.Ing. Hans Wocke began working on a larger jet-powered bomber. Initially a 25° swept-back wing was considered but wind-tunnel investigations indicated severe handling problems at low speed (as indeed proved to be the case with many early swept-wing aircraft). His revolutionary solution was to sweep the wing forward so that the tips would be the last section to stall and aileron control would be maintained. In view of this unconventional approach it was decided to build a prototype using existing components to test the theory. The result was the Junkers Ju 287 VI which took to the air on 16 August 1944.

Above: This view of the Junkers Ju 287 VI under construction at the Dessau factory in the summer of 1944 clearly shows the configuration of the forward-swept wing. The potential drawback of this layout is aeroelastic distortion at high speeds. In a swept-back wing, if the wingtip flexes up or down under aerodynamic loads, the airflow will tend to restore it to its normal position. However, with a swept-forward wing any deflection will tend to increase as the airflow now tends to further force the wingtip up or down depending on the angle of attack. In the worst case this could cause a structural failure and to prevent this the wing structure has to be strong enough to withstand such forces.

Opposite above: Apart from the wing and the new jet engines, the Junkers Ju 287 V1 was built from existing airframe components. The fuselage was that of a He 177 bomber adapted to take the wing structure and the tail assembly came from Ju 388 components. The strength requirements of the wing made it difficult to incorporate a retractable undercarriage so to save time a simple but rugged undercarriage was provided. The two main wheels came from a Ju 352 while the wheels on the two separate nose units came from a wrecked B-24 Liberator (who says recycling is a new concept!). All the wheels were enclosed in massive streamlined spats.

Opposite below: Mechanics prepare the Ju 287 for another test flight. For test purposes a crew of two was all that was required to operate the aircraft but the operational version would have had three crew. Two men are passing fuel into the main fuselage tank situated just forward of the wing root. Also visible is one of the two nose-mounted 1,984lb.s.t. Jumo 004B-1 turbojets while two further units were mounted in nacelles under the trailing edge of the wings. Take-off performance was boosted by a 2,645lb-thrust Walter 501 rocket pack under each engine which was jettisoned when airborne.

Above: During the Ju 287's flight test programme, a series of wool tufts were placed over the wings and fuselage and a cine camera mounted atop the fuselage in front of the fin to record the airflow variations. The lessons learnt were applied to the Junkers Ju 287 V2 which was much more representative of an operational bomber with a newly-designed fuselage based on that of the Ju 288 and was to be powered by no less than six 1,760lb.s.t. BMW 003A-1 turbojets, one pair mounted on the leading edge of each wing and single units on each side of the nose. Soviet forces overran the Junkers factory in April 1945 but that was not the end of the story (see Chapter 5). *AC*

There are few photos available showing the Ju 287 in the air but this slightly blurred image does clearly show the aircraft's unusual configuration. In fact the aircraft flew much as predicted and was reportedly pleasant to fly although the effects of aeroelastic distortion were noted on one occasion when it was dived to a speed of 404mph. *AC*

Chapter 2

Great Britain

In 1945, at the end of the Second World War, the front-line equipment of Bomber Command consisted of Lancaster and Halifax heavy bombers and Mosquito light bombers. After the end of hostilities the Halifax squadrons were quickly disbanded as the Lancaster was regarded as being the more efficient of the two, particularly in respect of bomb load. In 1944–5 some remarkable operations had been carried out by Lancasters carrying 12,000lb Tallboy or 22,000lb Grand Slam bombs. However, as early as 1943 the Air Staff were looking for an improved version with an eye to future operations against Japan for which a substantial increase in range would be required. The result was the Avro Lincoln (originally developed as the Lancaster Mk IV) which featured a new wing with increased span and a higher aspect ratio and was powered by four Merlin 85 engines rated at 1,750hp. Although the Lincoln could fly higher and

The RAF's standard heavy bomber in the immediate post-war era was the Avro Lincoln, developed from the famous Lancaster. In August 1945 the first unit to receive the Lincoln was 57 Squadron based at East Kirkby and one of their aircraft is shown here in the white-topped colour scheme applied to aircraft intended for service in the Far East against Japan. Although an improvement on the Lancaster, the Lincoln's performance was not good enough for the coming jet age.

further than a Lancaster, its cruising speed of around 200 knots was not significantly faster and was entirely inadequate in the era of jet fighters. Nevertheless, although too late to see action before VJ Day in August 1945, the Lincoln was produced in quantity and rapidly replaced the Lancasters of Bomber Command in the late 1940s and served with some twenty-nine squadrons as well as a number of training and trials units.

However, even as Lincoln production continued, the RAF was already looking for it to be replaced by jet bombers but it would obviously be several years before these could be developed and placed in service. Consequently in 1950 the RAF accepted the loan of a total of eighty-eight Boeing B-29 Superfortresses which became the Washington B.1 in British service. The first was delivered in March 1950 and they remained in service with Bomber Command until 1954. The Washington was very much a stopgap aircraft and American experience in Korea starkly illustrated that the B-29 could not be used for daylight bombing missions in the face of jet fighters such as the MiG-15 in the Korean War. Consequently there was never really any serious intention that the RAF's Washingtons would be used for strategic bombing missions against Soviet targets.

What was needed was a jet bomber which offered a reasonable chance of reaching a well-defended target and as early as 1946 the Air Staff issued a specification calling

Pending the introduction of jet bombers, in 1950 the RAF received enough Boeing B-29 Superfortresses from USAF stocks to equip eight squadrons and supplement the Lincolns of Bomber Command. In RAF service the aircraft was known as the Washington B.1.

for such an aircraft. Its origins were partly inspired by the spectacular success of the Mosquito in the light bomber role during the war. Despite carrying no defensive armament, the loss rate amongst the Mosquito bomber squadrons was significantly less than that of the four-engined heavy bombers. This was mainly because it could fly higher and faster than most enemy fighters and above the reach of effective anti-aircraft fire. This was even more true of the photo-reconnaissance Mosquitoes which roamed almost unchallenged over Europe from 1943 onwards. It was with this experience in mind that specification B.35/46 was issued for a jet bomber which would carry no defensive armament but would rely on speed at high altitudes to evade enemy defences. It called for a range of 3,350 miles carrying a 10,000lb bomb load and be capable of cruising at 500 knots (Mach 0.875) at altitudes of 50,000ft or above. In addition the aircraft was to be manoeuvrable at high speeds and altitudes.

Although such performance is almost routine for today's military aircraft, in 1946 it presented a considerable challenge to the British aviation industry and would require

The success of the Mosquito during the Second World War provided the inspiration for the new breed of jet bombers which would also rely on a combination of high speed at high altitude to evade enemy air defences. Even in the early jet age it was not outclassed and the last bomber variant (Mosquito B.35) served with Bomber Command until 1952–3 while the last photo-reconnaissance PR.34 (shown here) was not retired from front-line service until December 1955.

advances into unknown areas of aerodynamics and jet propulsion. Recognizing that this would require several years of development, but also facing an urgent need to equip the RAF with a jet bomber to replace the obsolescent piston-engined Lincoln, a separate specification was issued to the Belfast-based Short Brothers for an 'interim' jet bomber which would be relatively simple in concept and therefore capable of a short development period and rapid introduction into service. The result was the Short SA.4 Sperrin which flew in 1951, by which time it was recognized that something better was available in the form of the Vickers Valiant which had flown a few months earlier. Although originally rejected as a contender for the B.35/46, it was subsequently realized that the Valiant could be developed and placed in service at least two years ahead of the more advanced products from Avro and Handley Page and so it replaced the Sperrin as the interim bomber. First flown in 1951, it entered service at the start of 1955 and in the following year a Valiant successfully dropped Britain's first atomic bomb at the Maralinga range in South Australia.

On 8 August 1945 the nature of warfare had changed forever with the dropping of an atomic bomb on Hiroshima in Japan. A second bomb on Nagasaki a few days later forced Japan to surrender and the Second World War was ended. Although the bomb had been developed with a considerable contribution from British scientists and research establishments, in the post-war era the Truman administration decided that America would be the sole repository of the knowledge and facilities to develop and manufacture nuclear weapons and Britain was arbitrarily excluded (a situation not reversed until the mid-1950s). Consequently the British government decided that, despite the cost, Britain would have to develop its own independent nuclear capability and this programme was formally instituted by the then-Labour government in January 1947. This move was given further impetus by the rapidly-worsening relations with the Soviet Union and the latter's detonation of an atomic bomb in 1949.

It was one thing to develop an atomic bomb but it was another to deliver one against an enemy target. Although missiles were considered, overcoming the difficulties of developing a missile capable of carrying a 10,000lb warhead over at least 1,500 miles was quite beyond British technical and financial resources in the 1940s and 1950s. However, the bombers which would result from the B.36/45 specification were designed with this requirement in mind. Until 1949 the unspoken assumption was that the use of atomic weapons in a war would complement conventional forces to achieve victory but the advent of a Soviet bomb made such thinking redundant. Any future major conflict could result in a massive nuclear exchange which would leave both sides virtually destroyed, so that rather than prepare for a protracted and unwinnable campaign it was better to prevent such wars occurring. This was even more true following the development of thermonuclear H-bombs and it was this thinking which led to the concept of a nuclear deterrent, a role which the new

In the post-war era specifications for new jet bombers were built around the need to be able to deliver a nuclear weapon in the form of the Blue Danube atomic bomb. This was a 10-ton monster, the size of which determined the dimensions of the bomb bay in the forthcoming V-bombers. Although the first air-drop test did not take place until 1956, operational examples had been available from 1954. *AC*

bombers would successfully adopt from 1956 until it was passed on to the Royal Navy and its Polaris-equipped nuclear submarines in 1967.

The Valiant was so named after a poll among Vickers staff and followed the company tradition of alliterative names (e.g. Viking, Viscount). Avro wanted to give their Type 698 a name beginning with 'A' but by 1952 the Air Ministry decided that the new bombers should also have names beginning with 'V' which resulted in the Avro Vulcan and Handley Page Victor, and so the V-Bomber force was created. Prior to this, Air Ministry policy had been to name bombers after British and Commonwealth cities (hence Halifax, Lancaster, Lincoln) and the general principal was followed with the B-29 Washington. The one jet bomber which did follow this pattern was the English Electric Canberra (named after the Australian capital) which resulted from a 1944 requirement for a jet successor to the highly-successful Mosquito. Westland's chief designer, W.E.W. Petter, had already outlined a design for such an aircraft and moved to the English Electric Company which provided facilities for its development. The prototype flew in May 1949 and proved to have outstanding performance with only a few minor modifications required during the test programme. Less than two years later it entered RAF service as its first jet bomber and, as well as replacing

Mosquitoes, it also re-equipped several Lincoln and Washington squadrons. This effectively made it the *de facto* 'interim' jet bomber until the introduction of the Valiant in 1955. As well as its original role as a high-altitude bomber it was also produced as a photo-reconnaissance, training and ground-attack aircraft. It was also widely exported and built under licence in Australia and the USA.

In developing aircraft such as the Canberra and the V-bombers, the British aircraft industry produced aircraft which were the best of their type in the world. The concept of the high-speed high-altitude bomber remained valid until the mid-1960s when Soviet surface-to-air missile technology and fighter performance finally made interceptions possible. Even then, American experience with B-52 operations in Vietnam showed that a significant proportion of an attacking force could still get through, at least enough to still wreak unacceptable destruction. However, by that time the concept of a nuclear-armed strategic bomber had been almost totally replaced by the introduction of long-range ballistic missiles, each capable of carrying several independently-targeted nuclear warheads. Thus there was to be no like-for-like replacement for the V-bombers and, in RAF service at least, the bomber role is today filled by smaller multi-role aircraft such as the Eurofighter Typhoon and the new F-35B Lightning II.

The RAF's first jet bomber was the highly successful English Electric Canberra. The prototype (VN799) shown here took to the air on May 1949 and subsequently astounded observers at that year's Farnborough Air Show with its speed and manoeuvrability. This was down to a combination of the broad chord wing resulting in low wing loading and a pair of powerful new Rolls-Royce Avon RA.2 turbojets. Technically this was a Canberra B.1 produced to specification B.3/45 that envisaged a radar-based bomb-aiming system which, in the event, did not materialize. However, this explains the lack of a visual bomb aimer's compartment in the nose – a standard feature on the Canberra B.2 and subsequent bomber versions. Also noteworthy is the curved profile at the top of the tail fin which was subsequently revised to the more familiar squared-off fin. *APC*

Following on from the four prototypes was the first operational version, the Canberra B.2, of which the first (VX165) shown here flew on 21 April 1950. The most obvious external difference was the transparent nose for the bomb aimer and a crew of three was now standard (pilot, navigator, bomb aimer). Other improvements included more powerful Avon RA.3 engines, air brakes and provision for fitting wingtip fuel tanks. A total of 418 B.2s was produced, some of which were later converted to Canberra B.6 standard. *AC*

The Canberra's good performance at high altitude and its long-range capability made it ideal for the photo-reconnaissance role and this had been foreseen as early as 1946 when the new jet bomber was first envisaged. Specification PR.31/46 was issued and the prototype Canberra PR.3 flew on 20 March 1950. The aircraft here is the third production aircraft (WE137) which was one of a batch delivered to 540 Squadron at RAF Benson in December 1952. It wears the then-standard grey/black Bomber Command colour scheme. *APC*

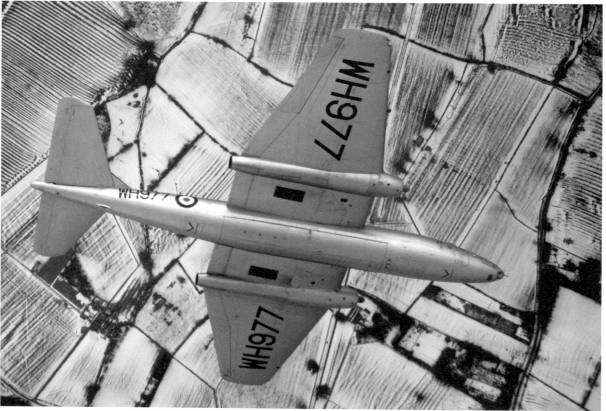

Opposite above: First flown on 26 January 1954, the Canberra B.6 had more powerful 7,500lb.s.t. Avon RA.7 engines and extra fuel capacity contained in integral leading-edge tanks. A total of 106 B.6s were built but many more were produced by upgrading earlier B.2s to the same standard. The Canberra's exceptional manoeuvrability is here demonstrated by a 9 Squadron aircraft over a snow-covered Lincolnshire landscape in the winter of 1955. *MoD*

Opposite below: The first unit to receive the Canberra B.6 was 101 Squadron at Binbrook in June 1954. By the end of 1955 a further six squadrons were equipped including 139 Squadron at Hemswell whose aircraft are shown lined up in review order, the tail fins carrying the squadron's red and white markings (note also the Lincolns in the background, probably belonging to 83 Squadron which was disbanded at the end of 1955). 139 Squadron operated Canberras until disbanded in December 1959, although it subsequently reformed in 1962 as a V-bomber squadron flying Handley Page Victors. *AC*

Above: The Canberra proved to be a most versatile aircraft and was eventually produced in no less than twenty-two variants. A total of 925 were built in the UK but another 48 were built under licence in Australia and 403 produced in America as the Martin B-57 (see Chapter 4). New and refurbished aircraft would be exported to fourteen air forces. Even by the end of 1954 variants other than those already described had flown including the T.4 trainer, the B.5 attack bomber which became the B(I).8, and the PR.7 shown here which made its debut at the 1954 Farnborough Air Show. This had actually flown on 16 August 1953 and pioneered the uprated Avons and integral leading-edge fuel tanks which were also applied to the B.6.

Above: Also flown in 1954 was the prototype Canberra B(I)8 (VX185). This was a specialized night intruder and ground-attack variant, very similar in concept to the Martin B-57B, and the obvious external change was the provision of an offset fighter-style canopy for the pilot. Internally the navigator/bomb aimer was accommodated in the nose. Other significant changes included underwing hardpoints for bombs and rockets and provision for a removable gun pack containing four 20mm cannon in the rear section of the bomb bay. Later Canberra developments included the Shorts-built Canberra PR.9 which first flew in 1958 and was the last variant in RAF service, only finally retiring in 2006. *AC*

Opposite above: A year after the end of the Second World War the Air Staff issued specification B.14/46 which called for a four-engined jet bomber to replace the piston-engined Avro Lincoln, then the RAF's front-line heavy bomber. The Short SA.4 design (later named the Sperrin) was selected and the first of two prototypes (VX158, shown here) flew on 10 August 1951. The specification called for the ability to carry a 10,000lb bomb load over 3,350nm at altitudes up to 45,000ft. At the same time it was to avoid advanced techniques and materials in order to simplify production and maintenance. The result was a conservative straight-wing design which nevertheless met most of the specification parameters and it proved to be manoeuvrable and easy to fly.

Opposite below: One unusual feature of the Sperrin was the location of the four Rolls-Royce Avon R.A.2 engines which were mounted in vertical pairs on either wing. This arrangement proved to offer low drag and good propulsive efficiency and the engines were actually mounted above and below the main spar which simplified the structural requirements and saved weight. The Sperrin was never ordered into production as the interim jet bomber role was more than adequately filled by the more advanced Vickers Valiant. However, both prototypes carried out valuable trials of equipment and techniques which were incorporated in the later V-bombers.

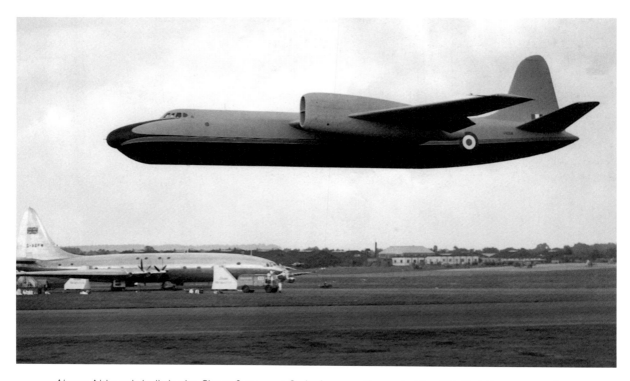

Above: Although built in the Short factory at Sydenham on the east side of Belfast, the runway there was not long enough for the Sperrin and so in August 1951 the prototype was taken by road to Aldergrove (10 miles west of Belfast) for its first flight and early testing. Although initially left in a natural metal finish, it was given this attractive colour scheme for its debut at the Farnborough Air Show only a few weeks later where it made a good impression (note the ill-fated Brabazon in the background). Nevertheless, by that time the prototype Valiant had already flown and the Sperrin was no longer required as an operational bomber. The second Sperrin (VX161) flew on 12 August 1952 and was initially engaged in dropping trials of dummy Blue Danube nuclear bombs and other weapons. It was eventually scrapped in 1957. *AC*

Opposite above: The arrangement of the engines also made the Sperrin easy to adapt as an engine test bed and in 1955 VX158 was fitted with 15,000lb.s.t. de Havilland Gyron jet engines in the lower half of each nacelle. Trials with this engine continued until the programme was cancelled in 1957 and the aircraft was scrapped in the following year. *PG.*

Opposite below: While the Short Sperrin had been ordered as a low-risk project, the Air Staff still wanted a bomber able to cruise above 50,000ft at a speed of 500 knots (Mach 0.875) carrying a nuclear weapon. Avro and Handley Page came up with designs incorporating advanced aerodynamic configurations but these would take time to develop. A Vickers design had been rejected as not being advanced enough but the company's chairman, Sir George Edwards, persevered and convinced the Air Staff that although relatively simple, his aircraft could meet most of the specification parameters and, crucially, could be available in a relatively short time. Consequently specification B9/48 was drawn up around the Vickers Type 660 design and the prototype (now named Valiant) flew on 18 May 1951 – some three months before the Short Sperrin. The prototype (WB210) is shown in its natural metal finish.

Opposite above: This air-to-air view of the prototype Valiant emphasizes its clean lines and shows the moderately swept wings (26°). This aircraft was powered by four Rolls-Royce Avon RA.3 turbojets rated at 6,500lb.s.t. which were installed in the thickened wing roots. This arrangement was typical of other British four-jet designs of the time and while it resulted in a very clean aerodynamic design it made the engines difficult to access for maintenance or replacement, in contrast to contemporary American jet bombers which carried their engines in nacelles or pods below the wing. WB210 was engaged in a busy test programme which unfortunately ended on 12 January 1952 when the aircraft was lost following an uncontrollable fire in the air during engine relight tests.

Opposite below: Despite the loss of the prototype, it had already shown the potential of the Valiant and work proceeded on the second prototype (WB215) which flew at Wisley on 11 April 1952. This featured more powerful Avon RA.7 engines rated at 9,500lb.s.t. and to cope with the increased mass of air flow the air intakes were enlarged as shown here. The shoulder-mounted wing allowed space for a capacious bomb bay in the centre fuselage which, as well as accommodating the standard Blue Danube nuclear weapon, could alternatively carry up to twenty-one 1,000lb conventional bombs. In this view the aircraft is fitted with optional underwing tanks which increased maximum range to 4,500 miles although with some reduction in bomb load. *PRM*

Above: The first of twenty-five production Valiant B.1s (WP199) flew on 22 December 1953 and the remainder were all delivered between December 1954 and July 1955. One of these (WP208) is shown at Vicker's Wisley airfield prior to handover to the RAF. At that time the Valiants were given a standard silver finish and the more familiar anti-radiation white colour scheme was only introduced towards the end of 1955 when operational nuclear weapons were about to become available. The first operational unit was 138 Squadron which formed at Gaydon in mid-1955 and subsequently it equipped nine other Bomber Command squadrons. *APC*

Above: For an 'interim' design the Valiant proved remarkably successful in its original role as a high-level strategic bomber and it subsequently also served as a tanker and photo-reconnaissance aircraft. A total of 107 (including three prototypes) were built before production ended in 1957. The last example was Valiant B(K).1 (XD875) shown taking off on its delivery flight from Wisley on 27 August 1957. *PG*

Opposite above: The increasing effectiveness of Soviet air defences in the early 1960s led to the Valiants being re-tasked to the low-level strike role for which they were not designed and the subsequent discovery of dangerous metal fatigue in the main spars led to the type being prematurely withdrawn from service at the end of 1964. Ironically this situation could have been avoided if the Valiant B.2 had been ordered into production. The sole prototype of this variant, the black-painted WJ954, flew on 4 September 1953 and was intended for the low-level target-marking role. The wing structure was considerably strengthened and this required that the undercarriage retracted rearwards into pods projecting beyond the trailing edge of the wing. Despite demonstrating excellent low-level performance, the RAF requirement was cancelled and the sole prototype was employed on various tests and trials before being scrapped in 1958. *AC*

Opposite below: Avro's design for a jet-powered strategic bomber was based around a thick delta wing, the first time such a configuration had been incorporated in a large aircraft. In order to provide practical experience of the delta wing Avro built a series of small research aircraft. The first of these was the single-seat Avro 707 (VX784) which first flew on 4 September 1949 and appeared in the static display at that year's Farnborough Air Show. Unfortunately its contribution to the research programme was very brief as it crashed during a test flight on the 30 September, killing its pilot 'Red' Esler.

Above: The Avro 707 prototype at the 1949 SBAC Show at Farnborough. This view shows the arrangement of the control surfaces on the trailing edge of the delta wing. The outboard pair acted as ailerons and the inner pair as elevators. Separate flaps were not fitted due to the high angle of attack of the delta wing at low speeds which generated the necessary lift and drag for which flaps were normally required on landing and take-off.

Opposite above: It was almost another year before the next 707 delta (VS790) flew on 6 September 1950. Designated the Avro 707B, it was also powered by a single 3,500lb.s.t. Rolls-Royce Derwent fed by a dorsal intake and was primarily intended for research into the low-speed handling qualities of the delta wing planform. In this role it gave excellent service and proved easy to handle throughout over 100 hours of test flying by a variety of civilian test pilots and service personnel.

Opposite below: It was found that at high speeds the airflow to the dorsal intake was disturbed by turbulence from the cockpit canopy, so in the Avro 707A (WD280 – first flight 14 June 1951) the dorsal intake was replaced by wing-root intakes. The aircraft was now more representative of the much larger Vulcan bomber, of which the prototype was then under construction, and was used extensively for research at high subsonic speeds.

Opposite above: The Avro 707C was a two-seat version of the 707A. Originally four were ordered for use by the RAF as trainers. However, only one (WZ744) was completed and this first flew at RAF Waddington on 1 July 1953 where it remained in the training role until transferred to the RAE Bedford for supersonic trials and was subsequently fitted with an early form of electronic fly-by-wire controls. It was only retired in 1967 together with the remaining active 707As (WZ736 and WD280). *PG.*

Opposite below: The first of the more advanced V-bombers to fly, the prototype delta-winged Avro Vulcan (VX770) is here being rolled out of the assembly hangar at Woodford prior to its maiden flight on 30 August 1952. Although the aircraft had been designed around the Bristol Olympus turbojet offering in excess of 10,000lb.s.t., delays in delivering flight-cleared engines meant that VX770 was initially fitted with four 6,500lb.s.t Rolls-Royce Avon RA.3 engines. Nevertheless it was still highly manoeuvrable for a bomber and test pilot 'Roly' Falk delighted the crowds at the 1952 Farnborough display by performing a complete roll. *PG.*

Above: The Vulcan prototype XV770 appeared again at the 1953 Farnborough SBAC show where it is shown touching down after another exciting display. Note the prominent airbrakes which are fully extended. Production Vulcans also carried a braking parachute as standard. *APC*

Above: The Vulcan's wing was initially a pure triangle as is clearly illustrated here. The delta planform meant that the wing roots could be up to 7ft thick to allow the engines to be completely buried in the wing but still retaining a low thickness/chord ratio for optimum aerodynamic efficiency. Visible are the doors of the capacious bomb bay which, like that of the Valiant, could accommodate a Blue Danube nuclear weapon or twenty-one 1,000lb conventional bombs. *PRM*

Opposite above: Although the large wing area of the Vulcan enhanced its handling at high altitudes, potentially damaging buffeting was experienced when carrying out high-G manoeuvres. Consequently the second prototype (VX777), which had first flown on 3 September 1953, was later (October 1955) fitted with a modified wing in which the sweepback of the inner leading edge was reduced from 52° to 42° and the outer leading edge had its sweepback increased to meet the wingtip profile. The result was the so-called 'kinked' delta which was adopted as standard and applied retrospectively to early production aircraft including XA889, the first production aircraft, which flew on 4 February 1955. *PRM*

Opposite below: By 1956 the Vulcan B.1 was in full production at Avro's Woodford factory near Manchester. These are part of the first production contract for twenty-five aircraft allocated serials from XA889 to XA913 including XA896 in the right foreground. Note that these aircraft are being completed with the revised kinked delta wing and are finished in natural aluminium paint. *PG*

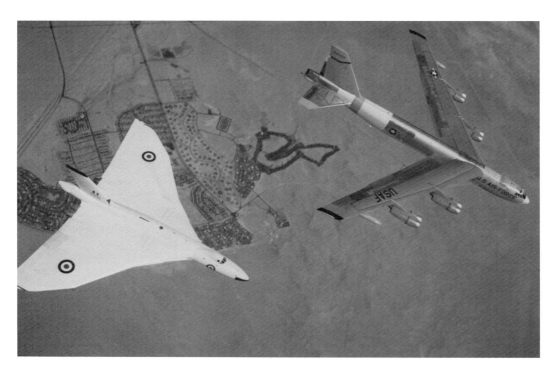

Opposite above: The Vulcan was destined to have a long and distinguished career with the RAF, most of which is outside the period covered by this book. In brief, the Vulcan B.1 entered service with 230 OCU in May 1956 and reached the first operational squadron (83) in July 1957. The Vulcan B.2 fitted with more powerful 17,000lb.s.t. or 20,000lb.s.t. Olympus turbojets entered service in 1960–1 and from 1963 was armed with the Blue Steel stand-off missile. From 1966 the V-force switched to low-level operations and in 1982, just as the last examples were being retired, a Vulcan of 44 Squadron finally carried out the type's only offensive operation when it dropped bombs on the airfield at Port Stanley in the Falklands in April 1982. This photo, taken during an exercise in America in 1962, shows a Vulcan B.2 in formation with a Boeing B-52 Stratofortress. Although the latter could carry a heavier bomb load, the Vulcan could fly higher and faster.

Opposite below: Handley Page's response to specification B.35/46 was the HP.80 Victor which would employ a complex crescent-shaped wing. In order to test the characteristics of this configuration a flying testbed was ordered in March 1948 under specification E.6/48. This was the Handley Page HP.88 and featured a 0.4 scale wing married to a Supermarine Swift fuselage (most accounts state that an Attacker fuselage was used and this was the original intention, but the basically similar Swift fuselage proved more suitable because the fuel system was compatible with a swept wing). Finished in a gloss royal blue colour scheme the HP.88 flew on 21 June 1951 but exhibited severe longitudinal stability which required several hours of testing and modification to overcome. Subsequently the aircraft was destroyed when it broke up in mid-air during a low level high speed run at Stansted on 26 August 1951, killing the pilot Douglas Broomfield. *AC*

Above: The loss of the HP.88 had little effect on the HP.80 Victor programme whose two prototypes were at an advanced stage of construction at Handley Page's Radlett works. The first of these (WB771) was completed by the end of May 1952 and was then dismantled and moved by road to Boscombe Down for flight testing as Radlett's runway was too short (it was later lengthened). However, it was not until 24 December that test pilot H.G. Hazelden was able to take WB177 on its maiden flight. Despite the advanced nature of the design no serious problems were encountered and at the time the futuristic science-fiction appearance of the aircraft generated much excitement in the popular press. The prototype was powered by four 7,500lb.s.t. Armstrong Siddeley Sapphires but production aircraft had the 11,050lb-thrust ASSa.7 Sapphire engines.

Above: For its appearance at the 1953 Farnborough Air Show the prototype Victor (WB771) was finished in this dramatic colour scheme comprising a matt black fuselage with red trim lines and silver-grey wings and tail surfaces. Now alongside the Valiant and Vulcan, the trio of V-bombers were a tribute to the capabilities of the British aircraft industry and a bold statement of Britain's determination at that time to remain a front-rank world power. Unfortunately WB771 was lost when doing some high-speed low-level test runs at Cranfield on 14 July 1954. Unforeseen tail flutter resulted in the entire tailplane breaking off and the aircraft ploughed into the runway, killing all on board. The cause was traced to an undetected error in the tailplane stress calculations (no computers in those days) but a modification to strengthen the fin/tailplane joint subsequently resolved the issue. *AC*

Opposite above: An early production Victor B.1 (XA922) banks away from the camera to display its crescent wing planform. This shape was adopted in order to deal with some of the problems associated with swept wings, including tip stalling leading to a dangerous pitch-up, and structural issues related to twisting forces. An incidental benefit was that the main spar structure was well forward of the centre of gravity so that the whole fuselage cross section aft of the rear spar was available for the military load. The Victor's bomb bay actually had twice the capacity of the Vulcan's and in service could carry up to thirty-six conventional 1,000lb bombs.

Opposite below: A line-up of Victor B.1s at Radlett awaiting delivering. The aircraft just behind the fence is the first production Victor B.1 (XA917) which flew on 1 February 1956 and this aircraft was notable for exceeding Mach 1 during a test flight in June 1957, then the largest aircraft to have achieved that feat. Victors entered operational service (with 10 Squadron) in April 1958 and, including the two prototypes and the later B.2 version (powered by Rolls-Royce Conway engines), a total of eighty-six were built. When the Valiant was prematurely withdrawn from service, all available Victor B.1s were converted to act as tankers. The large bomb bay provided significant space for additional fuel tanks and made the Victor ideal in this role. Later the remaining B.2s were also modified and the last of these was only retired in 1993. *APC*

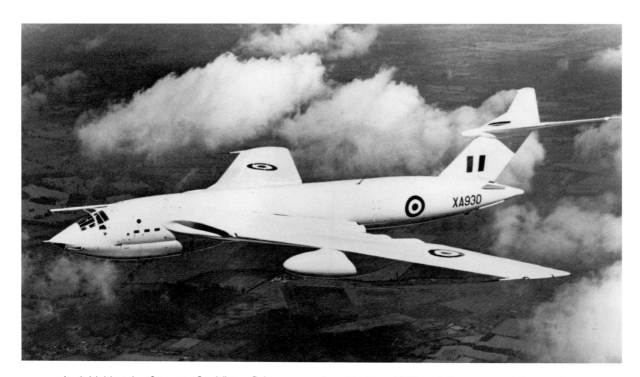

An initial batch of twenty-five Victor B.1s were ordered in June 1952 and these were delivered from February 1956 onwards. One of these was XA930 which is shown here in 1958 while carrying out in-flight refuelling trials for which it has underwing tanks and is fitted with a refuelling probe above the nose. Following the withdrawal of the Valiant tankers in 1964, the Victor force was gradually converted to act as tankers. Including two prototypes, a total of eighty-six Victors were built, including thirty-four of the improved B.2 powered by Rolls-Royce Conway engines. Victors were withdrawn from the bombing role in 1968 although some had been completed as strategic reconnaissance aircraft (SR.2) and served in that role until 1975. The tanker variants (K.1, K.1A and K.2) were not finally retired until 1993. *PRM*

Chapter 3

France

After the liberation of France in 1944 great efforts were made to resurrect the French aircraft industry which before 1940 had produced a variety of very good combat aircraft. However, the Armée de l'Air had concentrated on the production of twin-engined medium bombers and neglected to invest in four-engined strategic bombers so that only a couple of prototypes had flown by 1940 (the Bloch 135 and 162). During the period of occupation (1940–4) many French aircraft factories were committed to producing German aircraft such as the

By 1939 the French aircraft industry was starting to produce some advanced designs which bore comparison with the best of other nations. A good example was the Loiré et Olivier Leo 451 twin-engined medium bomber. Capable of over 300mph and carrying a 4,000lb bomb load, it began to enter service in late 1939 but was only available in small numbers when German forces invaded in 1940. Production continued in Vichy France and a total of 561 were eventually produced, some of which remained in service with the post-war Armée del'Air as late as 1957. In action the LeO 451 proved to be fast and manoeuvrable and was popular with its crews.

Junkers Ju 52, Arado Ar 196 and Focke-Wulf Fw 189 and in 1945 production of transport aircraft continued for a while. However, French designers were eager to apply the new jet technology although they were limited in their choice of power plants. Several aircraft were initially powered by captured Junkers Jumo 004 axial-flow turbojets although these proved unreliable. As a stopgap Hispano-Suiza obtained a licence to produce the 4,850lb.s.t. Rolls-Royce Nene, then the world's most powerful readily-available engine. Another potential power plant was based on the German BMW 003 engine from which the SNECMA Atar axial flow turbojet was eventually developed.

In the decade after 1944 France went on to produce an array of jet-powered prototypes but these were mostly fighters or research aircraft and only a few bombers were produced. Once again the emphasis was on light or attack bombers and there was no requirement for a strategic bomber, particularly as at that time France did not possess nuclear weapons. In fact at the end of the war the Armée de l'Air had inherited squadrons of Free French Halifaxes and Marauders but for financial reasons the government decided to stand down the bomber force and the aircraft were either scrapped or converted into transports. In respect of jet bombers, one promising project was the Aerocentre NC270 which featured a slightly swept wing and was to be powered by two Nene engines in nacelles at the wing roots. Maximum all-up weight was 25 tonnes (55,000lbs) and it would carry a 5-tonne (11,000lb) bomb load. Work commenced in 1946 but it was eventually realized that

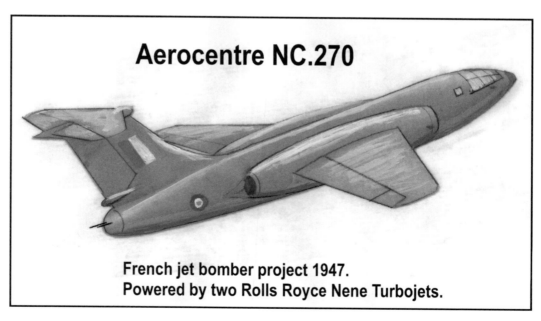

Aerocentre NC.270

French jet bomber project 1947.
Powered by two Rolls Royce Nene Turbojets.

An artist's impression of the Aerocentre (Nord) NC270. *ASM* the aircraft would be seriously underpowered given its size and weight and so for that reason, as well as budgetary constraints, the project was cancelled in 1947 when the prototype was 80 per cent complete.

Subsequent designs which actually flew included the Sud-Est SE.2410 Grognard and the Sud-Ouest SO.4000, both of which are described in the following pages. The only French-designed bomber originating from this period to enter operational service was the Sud-Ouest Vautour IIB, a light bomber based on this successful multi-role aircraft. As a postscript it is worth noting that France exploded its first atomic bomb in 1960 and from 1964 operational nuclear weapons were carried by the Dassault Mirage IV-A delta-winged bomber, the prototype of which had flown in 1959.

France's first jet bomber to fly and its first multi-engined jet aircraft was the Nord 1071. This strange-looking aircraft had a chequered history and a most unusual appearance. It was based on the Nord 1070, a twin piston-engined torpedo bomber produced in response to a French Navy requirement and which first flew on 29 May 1947. Effectively it had three fuselages, the outer two carrying the engines and supporting the tail surfaces while the crew of three occupied the centre fuselage. Although it flew well, performance was disappointing and the second prototype was modified to accept two Rolls-Royce Nene turbojets as illustrated. In this form it flew as the NC1071 from Toussus-le-Noble on 12 October 1948 but no further examples were ordered. AC

Above: This side view of the NC1071 prototype emphasizes its sheer size and the bulkiness of the extended pods which housed the Rolls-Royce Nene engines and carried the vertical tail surfaces.

Opposite above: Apart from the abortive NC.270, the Armée de l'Air also ordered another twin-jet bomber from SNCASO under the designation SO.4000. This was to feature a moderately swept wing (35°) and it was to be powered by two Rolls-Royce Nene turbojets mounted side-by-side in the rear fuselage. Initially two aerodynamically-representative manned scale models were ordered for test purposes but as early as 1947 it was decided that only these and a single prototype SO.4000 would be built for experimental and research purposes. The first of the scale models was the unpowered Sud-Ouest M-1 which is shown here mounted atop a carrier aircraft. After a series of flights in which basic aerodynamics were investigated while still attached, it was finally released for its first free flight on 26 September 1949.

Opposite below: The carrier aircraft for the M-1 was of great interest in its own right. It was in fact the sole prototype of the Heinkel He 274 high-altitude bomber which had been derived from the He 177, Germany's only operational four-engined heavy bomber. The He 177 was powered by four Daimler-Benz inline engines arranged in coupled pairs, a system which caused endless problems. The He 274 reverted to a more conventional four-engine layout together with a new high aspect-ratio wing and a lengthened fuselage. As the German company was fully occupied, design and construction of the He 274 was transferred to the French Farman company (Société Anonyme Usines Farman). The prototype was almost ready for flight in July 1944 when the factory at Suresnes was overrun by Allied forces and despite German attempts to destroy it, the damage was repaired and it was eventually flown in December 1945. Subsequently it was designated AAS-01A and used for high-altitude research and as a 'mother ship' for various experimental aircraft such as the SO.M-1. *AC*

Above: The Sud-Ouest SO M-2 (F-WFDR) was similar to the M-1 except that it was powered by a single Rolls-Royce Derwent turbojet and first flew on 13 April 1949, some months before the first free flight of the M-1. Both types were flown by Sud-Ouest's chief test pilot Jacques Guignard who took the M-2 up to speed of 621mph in May 1950. Note the unusual undercarriage arrangement with the main wheels under the centre fuselage and stabilizing outriggers at the wingtips.

Opposite above: The prototype SO.4000 (F-WBBL) was rolled out in March 1950. The two crew were accommodated in the pressurized nose section while the mid-mounted wing allowed an internal bomb bay intended to carry up to 4,000lbs of bombs. Defensive armament was projected as two single 20mm cannon carried in remotely-controlled barbettes on the wingtips. Estimates for maximum speed and service ceiling were 528mph and 42,000ft respectively. As tested on the M-2, the main undercarriage members retracted into the centre fuselage (outriggers were not fitted) and unusually each wheel was carried on an independent strut. Unfortunately this arrangement proved too weak and it collapsed on 23 April 1950 during taxying trials causing considerable damage. However, it was repaired and the SO.4000 took off on its first and only flight on 15 March 1951. This proved to be a disaster – the aircraft was obviously underpowered and was unstable in the air while on landing the undercarriage collapsed again. As a result the whole project was abandoned. *AC*

Opposite below: Produced to a 1948 specification for a jet-powered attack bomber, the Sud-Est SE.2410 Grognard first flew on 30 April 1950. In common with many French designs of the period it incorporated several unusual features, the most obvious of which was the installation of the two Hispano-Suiza Nene 101 turbojets which were mounted one above the other in the rear fuselage with the intake ducting above and behind the cockpit. This arrangement was intended to leave a clean airflow over the mid-mounted wing which was swept at 47°. However, this in turn necessitated that the undercarriage retracted into fuselage which left little room for a weapons bay and an armament of bombs and rockets would have been mostly carried underwing. *AB*

Opposite above: The name Grognard translates as 'Grumbler', a nickname for a soldier of Napoleon's Old Guard. The original 1948 Armée de l'Air specification called for a ground-attack bomber but was later altered to include an all-weather fighter role. No production order for the single-seat SE.2410 was forthcoming and the sole prototype, shown here with its braking parachute deployed after landing, was used for various weapon trials and tests before being scrapped in 1954.

Opposite below: A second prototype to a modified design was designated SE.2415 Grognard II and first flew on 14 February 1951. This seated a crew of two in tandem in a lengthened fuselage and the wing sweep was reduced to 32°. Unfortunately this aircraft was badly damaged in an emergency landing following a fire indication (which subsequently proved to be false) and was not repaired. The airframe, stripped of engines and other equipment, was expended as target in firing tests.

Above: A view of the SE.2415 Grognard II showing the arrangement of the two Nene engines in the rear fuselage. A development of this aircraft was the SE.2418 attack bomber which reverted to the 47° swept wing of the Grognard I and would have been powered by two 6,250lb.s.t. Rolls-Royce Tay turbojets. Work on this had commenced in 1952 when the whole Grognard programme was cancelled in favour of the more promising Sud-Ouest Vautour.

Above: In 1951 the Armée de l'Air issued a specification for a jet combat aircraft which would be able to perform several operational functions including all-weather interceptor, low-level ground attack and light bomber. Drawing on their experience with the SO.4000, Sud-Ouest proposed a swept-wing twin jet powered by a pair of axial-flow turbojets and an order for three prototypes was subsequently placed. Known as the SO.4050 Vautour II, the first prototype flew on 16 October 1952. This was the two seat all weather fighter version known as the Vautour IIN and was followed on 16 December 1953 by the prototype Vautour IIA and finally by the Vautour IIB bomber version on 5 December 1954. Photo shows the prototype Vautour IIN.

Opposite above: The single-seat Vautour IIA shown here was the attack version of this versatile aircraft and illustrates the tandem main wheel undercarriage arrangement with stabilizing outrigger wheels which retracted into the engine nacelles. Armament comprised four nose-mounted 30mm cannon and an internal weapons bay could accommodate up to 4,500lbs (2040kg) of bombs or a retractable rocket pack with 116 x 68mm rockets. Additional ordnance could be carried on underwing hardpoints. Apart from the prototype and two development aircraft a total of thirty Vautour IIA were delivered but they were not allocated to Armée de l'Air operational units and eighteen were exported to Israel.

The Vautour IIB bomber version flew in December 1954 and was followed by a single pre-production and forty production aircraft (four of which were delivered to Israel). The prototype was powered by two 8,000lb.s.t. Armstrong Siddeley Sapphire axial flow turbojets but production aircraft reverted to the improved Atar 101E-3 rated at 7,710lb.s.t. The Vautour IIB entered service in 1956/7 with the 92me Escadre de Bombardement and formed part of France's Force de Frappe (Strike Force) until replaced by the Mirage IV-A in the mid-1960s.

Chapter 4

United States

By the end of the Second World War the United States had the largest bomber fleet in the world by a considerable margin. In Europe it had fought the strategic bomber campaign with B-17 Flying Fortresses and B-24 Liberators but by 1945 these had been almost entirely replaced in the Pacific theatre with much more sophisticated B-29 Superfortresses. Not only in numbers was America superior but it was the sole possessor of the atomic bomb. Inevitably the size of the bomber fleet

In 1945 the B-29 Superfortress was the most advanced strategic bomber in the world and a total of 3,960 had been delivered when production ceased in May 1946. In the post-war era it was followed by the B-50 (originally the B-29D) which had more powerful Pratt & Whitney R-4360 Wasp Major engines in revised nacelles and could also be distinguished by a taller fin. There were also numerous detail improvements including a lighter but stronger wing. The first B-50A was flown in July 1947 and this was the first new bomber type to be delivered to the recently-formed SAC where it supplemented, but not entirely replaced, the B-29. The major production version was the B-50D shown here of which 222 were ordered. When later replaced by new jet bombers, many were converted to refuelling tankers as the KB-50D and from 1957 were upgraded to KB-50J standard by the addition of two J47 turbojets mounted in underwing pods. The last of these were still in service over Vietnam as late as 1965.

declined rapidly in the immediate post-war era but by 1948 the establishment of the so-called Iron Curtain and the Soviet blockade of Berlin served to heighten tension between the great powers and the detonation of a Soviet atomic bomb in 1949 set in motion a nuclear arms race in which the jet bomber would be a key element.

The strengthening of the American bomber force was facilitated by organizational changes to the structure of US air power. Historically, military aviation in the United States had been the preserve of the US Army and Navy, with no separate air force as in the United Kingdom. In 1941 the previous US Army Air Corps became the US Army Air Force (USAAF), virtually an independent force but still tied to the Army in matters such as uniform and military discipline as well as budget appropriations. Finally on 18 September 1947 it separated entirely from the Army and became the United States Air Force (USAF). This enabled the new service to undergo a complete reorganization which included the setting-up of Strategic Air Command (SAC), responsible for the operational control of all the strategic bomber squadrons, and Tactical Air Command which controlled the fighter and attack bomber squadrons

One new bomber which entered service in 1948 with SAC was the massive six-engined Convair B-36 but this was still powered by piston engines (although

The other major addition to SAC in the late 1940s was the massive Convair B-36, shown here for comparison alongside a B-29. Later known unofficially as the 'Peacemaker', this had originated in 1940 with a requirement for a bomber capable of attacking European targets from US home bases. As the war progressed it was also seen as a means of reaching Japanese targets and was accorded a higher priority although the prototype did not fly until 8 August 1946 (one year to the day after the first atomic bomb had been dropped on Hiroshima). Deliveries of operational B-36s to SAC began in June 1948 and eventually a total of 383 were built. Until the advent of the Boeing 747 in 1970, the Convair B-36 was by far the largest and heaviest aircraft ever built.

later augmented by jet engines). However, despite its substantial fleet of piston-engined bombers, the USAAF had been quick to recognize the potential of the jet engine to improve bomber performance In 1944 the aviation industry was invited to present proposals for a bomber capable of cruising at 450mph (maximum speed 550mph) at 45,000ft and having a range of 3,500 miles. This drew responses from several companies and in 1945 four were selected to proceed with development of prototypes. North American and Convair were given contracts for their four-engined medium bomber designs which became the B-45 Tornado and XB-46 respectively while Boeing and Martin were to work on larger six-engined projects (B-47 Stratojet and XB-46).

Even while this was in progress the Air Force issued a further request in 1946 for a new ultra-long range bomber with a combat radius of 5,000 miles. Boeing responded with a straight-wing design powered by six turboprops but this offered little improvement over the B-36 and so the design was refined until by 1950 it had

In order to improve performance a B-36 was fitted with four jet engines mounted under the outer wing in paired pods and in this form was produced as the B-36D from 1949 while many earlier models were converted to this configuration. The B-36D could lift a maximum bomb load of 84,000lbs, cruise at 400mph and had a service ceiling of 43,000ft. Illustrated here is the strategic reconnaissance version, the RB-36D. In the early 1950s the B-36 formed the backbone of the SAC nuclear-armed bomber force, equipping up to ten combat wings, until it began to be replaced by the B-52 Stratofortress in 1955. The last operational B-36 was retired in February 1959.

morphed into a swept-wing long-range bomber powered by no less than eight jet engines. This eventually flew in 1952 as the B-52 Stratofortress, which proved to be an outstanding success and remains in front-line service today.

While the B-47 and B-52 were to provide the backbone of SAC in the period under review in this book, the American aircraft industry had not really provided an outstanding light or tactical bomber. The North American B-45 Tornado was ordered into production but was not particularly advanced for its time. Significantly, it was completely outclassed by the British English Electric Canberra which was subsequently built in America as the Martin B-57, deliveries commencing in mid-1953. This went on to have a successful career and was heavily involved in the Vietnam War.

It was not only the Air Force which developed jet bombers. The US Navy saw the new USAF and its SAC as a threat to its own position, particularly with regards to funds for its programme of new *Forrestal*-class super carriers. Consequently it

The US Navy was determined to have a nuclear strike capability and between 1948 and 1952 maintained two squadrons equipped with specially-modified Lockheed P2V-3C Neptune bombers. Basically a land-based maritime patrol aircraft, it was able to take off from the large *Midway*-class carriers carrying a 10,000lb 14-kiloton nuclear weapon using RATOG boosters as illustrated here aboard the USS *Franklin D Roosevelt* (CV43). There was no question of the Neptune being able to land back on the carrier and it would have to find a suitable friendly airfield – assuming, of course, that it had survived an attack on Soviet territory. A significant problem was that when deployed the Neptunes had to be parked on deck and consequently other aircraft could not be operated.

worked hard to develop its own carrier-based nuclear strike capability, even going as far as equipping a squadron of land-based Neptune patrol bombers with RATOG boosters to allow them to take off from (but not land on) an aircraft carrier. This was a desperate measure and if flown in anger would have resulted in one-way suicide missions. A slightly better proposition was the North American AJ-1 Savage which was basically a twin piston-engined attack bomber with a jet engine in the rear fuselage, but again this was unlikely to have succeeded against jet fighter opposition. The ultimate Navy jet bomber was the swept-wing twin-jet Douglas A3D Skywarrior which first flew in 1952. Unusually its performance was such that a modified version entered USAF service as the B-66 Destroyer in 1956.

By the end of the period under review in this book even more advanced bombers such as the supersonic B-58 Hustler were under development but, as with British experience, much of the bomber's traditional role came to be carried out by a combination of missiles and modern multi-role aircraft. Despite the introduction of advanced strategic bombers such as the B-1 and the B-2, the USAF still has a substantial inventory of B-52s whose service life dates back to the 1950s and seems set to continue into the 2050s!

In 1943 the Douglas company submitted a proposal for an extremely advanced medium bomber in which two 1,325hp Allison V-1710-125 engines were mounted within the fuselage and connected by shafts to a pair of tail-mounted contra-rotating propellers. The clean high aspect-ratio wing carried a pair of streamlined remotely-controlled turrets each containing two 0.5in machine guns. The nose section housed the bombardier/navigator and the pilot and co-pilot/gunner were accommodated in separate cockpits under clear-view bubble canopies. Normal bomb load comprised four 2,000lb bombs and maximum speed was just over 400mph. The Army Air Force was very enthusiastic and two prototypes were ordered as the XB-42 Mixmaster, the first (serial 43-50224) being completed in May 1944.

The second prototype (43-50225), which flew on 1 August 1944, was later fitted with a more conventional single canopy as shown here. As a demonstration of its capabilities it was flown from Long Beach, California, to Bolling Field, DC in 5 hours 17 minutes averaging 433.6mph in early December 1945. Unfortunately it was then lost in an accident a few days later.

Despite the impressive performance of the XB-42, the Air Force did not order it in to production, preferring to wait for the more advanced jet bombers now in prospect as the Second World War drew to a close. However, it was decided to adapt the remaining XB-42 for research purposes by adding a pair of 1,600lb.s.t. Westinghouse 19XB-2A turbojets below the wings. In this form the aircraft was redesignated the XB-42A and flew on 27 May 1947, spending the next two years undergoing various tests and trials before being struck off charge. It still exist today in the collection of historic aircraft of the National Air & Space Museum, Washington DC. *WC*

Above: The design of the piston-engined Douglas XB-42 was such that it was relatively easy to adapt it for jet power. The idea was discussed as early as 1943 and in March 1944 a contract was issued for two jet-powered XB-43s and in fact the first of these (44-61508) was constructed using the airframe of an XB-42 which had been originally built for static testing purposes. Two 3.750lb.s.t General Electric TG-180 (J35-GE-3) turbojets fed by flush intakes set in the fuselage sides replaced the Allison piston engines and these exhausted through long tail pipes. The removal of the propellers meant that the ventral fin was not required and a new tall upper fin was added. Problems with the new jet engines delayed a first flight until 17 May 1946 and the XB-43 was subsequently found to be slightly underpowered. Nevertheless, it was 100mph faster than the original XB-42 and had the distinction of being America's first jet bomber.

Opposite above: Despite the good potential of the XB-43, by the time the prototypes had flown the Air Force had already decided that it wanted something larger and was looking at various four-engined designs and so no production contracts were forthcoming. This view of the second XB-43 (44-61509) emphasizes the exceptionally clean lines of the design. This aircraft was used as an engine testbed and one of its J35s was replaced by a General Electric J47. The first XB-43 was damaged in an accident February 1951 and was subsequently used as a source of spares to keep the second aircraft flying until 1953.

Opposite below: The competition to provide a four-engined jet bomber was won by North America with the B-45 Tornado. This was a very conservative design with straight wings and tail surfaces and four 4,000lb-thrust Allison (General Electric) J35-A-4 turbojets arranged in pairs in underwing nacelles. The crew of four consisted of two pilots in tandem under a fighter-type canopy, a bombardier/navigator in the nose and a rear gunner. Three prototypes were ordered in 1945 and the first of these flew on 17 March 1947 by which time it had already been ordered into production. Shown here is the first prototype (45-59479) at North American's Los Angeles facility while undergoing initial flight testing.

Above: A total of ninety-six B-45As were produced and all were eventually fitted with 4,000lb thrust General Electric J47 engines but although these functioned well in other aircraft (notably the F-86 Sabre) they caused endless problems in the Tornado. Nevertheless, the B-45A entered service with the 47th Bombardment Group in November 1948, making it the USAF's first operational jet bomber. The aircraft's great attribute was its ability to carry up to 22,000lbs of bombs albeit only over a limited range. *USAF*

Opposite above: By the time that the B-45 entered service it was being overshadowed by the Boeing B-47 and subsequent production orders were reduced. However, when the Korean War broke out it was decided to convert around forty B-45As for the nuclear strike role and equipped with these, the 47th Bomb Group was dispatched to Europe where it was based at RAF Sculthorpe from June 1952 until 1957. This photo shows a line-up of the Group's aircraft at Langley AFB, VA, in May 1952 prior to their onward flight across the Atlantic. The Group was disbanded on its return in 1957 at which point the B-45A was withdrawn from front-line service although some were converted as target tugs (TB-45A) and others were used as engine test beds.

Opposite below: For the flight across the Atlantic the 47th Bomb Group's B-45As were equipped with additional long-range fuel tanks suspended below the engine nacelles as illustrated here by one of their aircraft departing from Langley AFB.

Opposite above: This is the first production B-45C Tornado which featured more powerful 5,200lb-thrust J47-GE-13 engines and was equipped with wingtip fuel tanks. Intended as a tactical bomber, it had a strengthened airframe and a new framed canopy for the pilots replaced the fighter-type bubble canopy of the earlier versions.

Opposite below: Only ten B-45Cs were built but thirty-three derivative photo-reconnaissance versions designated RB-45C were produced, these being easily recognizable by the solid nose which replaced the bombardiers glazed compartment. First flown in April 1950, the RB-45C entered service in 1951 and some were immediately deployed to Japan where they replaced the obsolete RB-29s which had suffered at the hands of the enemy MiG-15s. RB-45Cs were also deployed to Europe and at one time four aircraft were seconded to the RAF who in 1952–4 flew them on intelligence gathering missions over Soviet territory. USAF RB-45Cs were active until 1958 when they were retired.

Above: A rival for the contract won by North American was Convair's Model 109, later designated XB-46. Although similar in overall configuration it gave the appearance of being more refined with a long slim fuselage and a wide-span high aspect-ratio wing. It was also powered by four Allison J35 engines housed in pairs in underwing nacelles. Despite its streamlined appearance, its top speed of 545mph was slower than that of the B-45 Tornado (579mph) and its bomb load was considerably less. Originally three prototypes were ordered in February 1945 but at Convair's request funding for the last two was diverted to another company project, the XA-44.

Above: The XB-46 was first flown on 2 April 1947 but it was basically only an aerodynamic shell, being devoid of any military equipment such as defensive armament and radar bombing systems. Although the pilot reported good handling qualities, subsequent testing revealed several problems including engine de-icing, tail vibration and oscillations when the spoilers were deployed. The XB-46 programme was cancelled in August 1947 but flight testing continued until 1949 when the aircraft was grounded. An interesting feature of the aircraft was that all the control systems were pneumatically driven instead of the more usual hydraulic or electric systems.

Opposite above: An artist's impression of the futuristic-looking Convair XA-44 (later redesignated XB-53) whose main feature was a swept-forward wing based on German wartime research. Power was to be provided by three J35 turbojets and bomb load was estimated as 12,000lbs. Top speed was projected at 580mph and service ceiling at 44,000ft. Although work began on the two prototypes, the project was halted before any significant progress had been made and it was finally cancelled in 1949. *WC*

Opposite below: As builders of the B-17 Flying Fortress and B-29 Superfortress, Boeing was eager to be in at the ground floor of jet bomber development and responded to a 1943 USAAF requirement for a jet bomber with a scaled-down B-29 powered by four wing-mounted jet engines (Boeing Model 424). To meet a revised requirement in 1944 the engines were moved into the forward fuselage to reduce drag and a preliminary contract was awarded under the designation XB-47. Realizing the significance of swept-wing technology discovered in May 1945 by Boeing engineers in Germany, work on the XB-47 was halted while it was redesigned with the new wing shape. Given the limited power available from the early jet engines, their number was increased to six and they were moved from the fuselage to underwing pods. In this form the design became the Model 450 and two prototypes were ordered in April 1946. The first of these (serial number 46-0065) is shown being rolled out on 12 September 1947. *USAF*

Opposite above: The XB-47 Stratojet caused an absolute sensation when it appeared in 1947, its sleek lines looking like nothing else flying at that time. The mounting of the engines in underslung pods was entirely new but apart from allowing easy access for maintenance their positioning and the swept-forward pylon mounting of the inboard engines made a significant contribution to reducing stresses on the wing in flight. The shoulder-mounted, thin, high aspect-ratio wing was swept at 35° and the shape and position of the engine pods left no room for undercarriage members. Consequently a tandem configuration was adopted for the main wheels with the two wheel bogies retracting into bays in front of and behind the bomb bay. Stabilizing outriggers retracted into the lower sides of the inner engine pods.

Opposite below: The XB-47 prototype was first flown on 17 December 1947, exactly 43 years to the day after the Wright brothers' first powered flight, and was powered by six 3,750lb.s.t. General Electric J35 engines. The heavy XB-47 took some stopping after landing or an aborted take-off, particularly on a wet runway, so a braking parachute was fitted as standard and this was often deployed before the aircraft touched down.

Above: The second prototype XB-47 (46-0066) flew on 21 July 1948 and differed in that it was powered by six 5,200lb.s.t. J47-GE-11 engines, as were the ten pre-production B-47As which followed. Despite its size, the B-47 Stratojet was operated by a crew of only three. The pilot and co-pilot sat in tandem under a fighter-type canopy while a bombardier/navigator sat in the nose compartment. The first B-47A (49-1900 shown here) was delivered in July 1950 but like its sister-ships was used for testing and training. The rows of ports immediately in front of the fuselage national markings are the exhaust for the RATOG system which was needed to accelerate the heavily-laden aircraft on take-off.

Above: The first full production version was the B-47B of which 399 were produced, including eight built by Lockheed and ten by Douglas. These two companies would subsequently build significant numbers of the later B-47E. The B-47B became operational with the 306th (Medium) Bomb Wing in the summer of 1951 and the outbreak of the Korean War added urgency to the rate at which SAC squadrons could be equipped. *USAF*

Opposite above: Coincidently with the B-47B becoming operational, the USAF also introduced the Boeing KC-97 Stratotanker into service in 1951. Based on the Stratofreighter transport, the KC-97E was able to carry out in-flight refuelling using the Boeing-designed flying boom system and the B-47B carried the necessary receiving equipment a standard. This system enabled SAC to maintain B-47s on airborne standing alert and for this purpose no less than twenty KC-97s were allocated to each B-47 Wing of forty-five bombers. *USAF*

Opposite below: The main production version was the B-47E and no less than 1,241 were built by Boeing, Lockheed and Douglas. It was powered by 6,000lb.s.t. (7,200lb.s.t. with water injection) J47-GE-25 engines and the remotely-controlled tail turret now mounted twin 20mm cannon with an A-5 fire-control system instead of twin 0.5in machine guns. The crew were also provided with ejector seats (although the bombardier's fired downwards) and the fixed 18-unit RATOG installation was replaced by a jettisonable 19- or 33-rocket pack below the rear fuselage. Most of the earlier B-47Bs were subsequently modified to this standard. Production of the B-47E ended in February 1957 at which time there were around 1,800 Stratojets in service with SAC and the last of these was not retired from operational service until 1966.

Above: In addition to the bomber version, a further 240 RB-47E photo-reconnaissance variants were also delivered from August 1953 onwards. These had a slightly lengthened nose and no less than eleven cameras were installed at various points in the fuselage and the former bomb bay. The fixed 18-rocket RATOG installation was retained as this version operated at lower take-off weights than the standard B-47E and did not need the bigger rocket packs.

Opposite above: Originally developed to the same operational requirement which led to the Boeing B-47, the Glenn Martin Company produced a much more conservative design – the Model 223 (Air Force designation XB-48). Although also powered by six jet engines (Allison J35-A-5, rated at 3,850lb.s.t.), these were carried in triple nacelles under the wide-span (108ft 4in), shoulder-mounted straight wing. A crew of three was housed in the nose of the rather tubby fuselage which at least allowed for a spacious bomb bay capable of carrying up to 20,000lbs of bombs. *USAF*

Opposite below: The prototype Martin XB-48 (45-59585) taking off on its maiden flight from the company airfield at Baltimore, Maryland, on 22 June 1947. Once airborne it made a short transit flight to NAS Patuxent River but on landing an issue with the brakes caused all four main wheel tyres to burst. Fortunately the damage was relatively slight and easily repaired. However, by the spring of 1948 it was apparent that the rival B-47 would offer substantially better performance than the Martin XB-48. Consequently, although a second prototype (45-59586) was flown on 16 October 1948, the Air Force had already decided to award production contracts to the Boeing product. Flight testing continued for a while but the first prototype was grounded in 1949 and cannibalized for spares to keep the second flying before that was also retired in 1951. *USAF*

Opposite above: A ground view of the XB-48 showing to advantage the configuration of the triple engine nacelles, sometimes referred to as gondolas. These were designed to contribute aerodynamic lift and the ducts between the J35 engines were intended to provide cooling air through the whole installation which also featured adjustable tailpipes. *USAF*

Opposite below: A notable feature of the XB-48 was the use of a tandem-wheel main undercarriage supplement by outrigger wheels which retracted into the engine nacelles. Although not fitted to the prototypes, there was provision for a remotely-controlled tail-mounted twin 0.5in machine-gun mounting. In many ways the XB-48 was equivalent to the British Short Sperrin which was originally ordered as insurance in case the V-bombers were not successful. A similar concept applied to the XB-48 in respect of the advanced but unproved Boeing B-47. *USAF*

Above: The advantage of the tandem-wheel undercarriage was that it retracted into the fuselage as the thin wings of the early American jet bombers would not accommodate a conventional undercarriage. However, it was an advanced concept at the time and so was tested on a converted Martin Marauder under the designation B-26H. The name 'Middle River Stump Jumper' painted on the nose refers to the location of Martin's airfield at Middle River. The tandem undercarriage was also adopted by the Boeing B-47 although it is not recorded if their engineers were afforded access to data from the Martin testbed.

Above: Although the Boeing B-47 amply met the requirements of SAC, Tactical Air Command had a requirement for a fast light bomber. In 1945 Martin put forward their Model 234 which, unusually, was powered by three General Electric J47-GE-013 engines. This was initially allocated the Air Force designation XA-45 (indicating the attack role) but this was changed to XB-51 when two prototypes were ordered in June 1946.

Opposite above: The prototype XB-51 (46-685) as rolled out in the summer of 1949. The engines were carried in pods mounted low down the forward fuselage and a third engine was to be in the rear fuselage fed by a dorsal intake. As shown here the dorsal intake is blanked off, indicating that the third engine has yet to be installed although it was fitted for the first flight which took place on 28 October 1949. The crew of two consisted of the pilot housed under the fighter-type clear-view canopy and a navigator/bombardier in a separate compartment in the fuselage behind the cockpit. The latter would operate the short-range navigation and bombing system which was planned for operational aircraft.

Opposite below: Technicians stand by as the J35 turbojets are started prior to a test flight. The XB-51 also used the tandem main wheel undercarriage configuration developed by Martin. This, together with the fuselage-mounted engines, left the swept wing clear of any attachments, reducing drag and improving efficiency. In fact the XB-51 was the fastest of the contemporary USAF jet bombers with a top speed of 645mph at sea level. *USAF*

Above: In common with other contemporary American jet bombers, the XB-51 needed rocket assistance for take-off with a heavy load as demonstrated here by the prototype. The initial specification called for the ability to carry a 4,000lb bomb load but a maximum load of 10,400lbs was possible although this included the use of external hardpoints. A fixed nose-mounted battery of no less than eight 20mm cannon was planned for production aircraft. *USAF*

Opposite above: An novel feature of the XB-51 was the rotary bomb bay set into the lower fuselage. This arrangement was pioneered by the Martin company and eliminated the problems experienced when conventional drag-inducing bomb doors were opened at high speed. *USAF*

Opposite below: The second XB-51 (46-686), which flew on 17 April 1950, was extensively employed in armament trials including operation of the rotary bomb bay which proved very successful. In fact the aircraft flew well and had an excellent performance and there appears to be no clear reason why it was not ordered into production. Unfortunately the second prototype was lost while performing low-level aerobatics on 9 May 1952. Its sister-ship (46-685) continued to fly for research purposes but crashed on take-off from El Paso on 25 March 1956. *USAF*

Opposite: The spectacular display by the English Electric Canberra prototype at the 1949 Farnborough Air Show prompted considerable interest from foreign air forces. In particular the USAF sent a mission to the UK in 1950 to examine the aircraft and this resulted in an invitation to send a Canberra to America for a comparative evaluation against other current light bombers. Accordingly an early production Canberra B.2 (WD932) was dispatched to the States on 21 February 1951 and in so doing became the first jet aircraft to make an unrefuelled direct crossing of the Atlantic. After successfully completing the evaluation process at Andrews AFB, the aircraft was flown to Glenn Martin's Baltimore airfield where Roly Beamont gave this impressive demonstration.

Above: WD932 at Andrews AFB in late February 1951 while taking part in comparative trials against the Martin XB-51, the North American B-45 Tornado and AJ-1 Savage and the Douglas B-26 Invader. The British jet completely outclassed its rivals, particularly in terms of manoeuvrability, and as a result it was selected for USAF service although it would be built under licence by the Glenn Martin company as the Martin B-57.

Above: English Electric provided two aircraft (WD932, WD940) to Glenn Martin for familiarization and flight testing and the first Martin-built B-57A (52-1418) flew on 20 July 1953. Although externally similar, the American aircraft featured several changes including the use of Wright J65 engines (licence-built Armstrong Siddeley Sapphires) and the installation of a rotary bomb bay as originally developed for the unsuccessful XB-51. The whole airframe was re-engineered to American standards and USAF radio, bombing and navigation equipment was installed.

Opposite above: Although it had taken two years to develop the Martin B-57 as a wholly American product, by 1953 substantial orders had been placed and the Martin factory at the Middle River airfield already had an efficient production line set up. Its capacity was illustrated by the fact that Martin produced no less than seventy-five B-57 variants in the first full year of production while English Electric delivered only twenty-five aircraft to the RAF in the corresponding period. *USAF*

Opposite below: Martin's initial production contract called for eight B-57As and sixty-seven RB-57As. The latter differed mainly in that a camera bay was installed aft of the rotary bomb bay. The first RB-57A (52-1426) was rolled out towards the end of 1953 and was finished in the then standard all black colour scheme with red serials and lettering. *USAF*

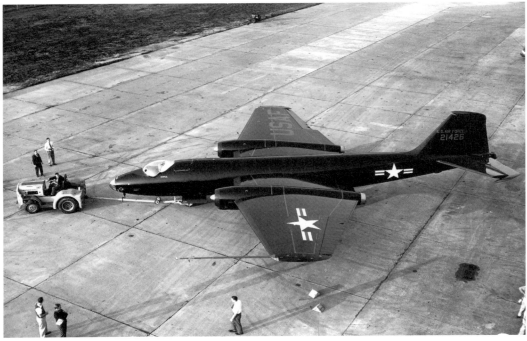

Above: The first operational unit to receive the RB-57A was the 363rd Tactical Reconnaissance Wing at Shaw AFB, South Carolina, where the new jets replaced B-26 Invaders. Here the wing puts up an impressive four-ship formation and the high-gloss nature of the paint scheme is illustrated by the fact that the apparent checkerboard markings on the tailplanes are actually reflections of a red and white pattern painted on the vertical fins. *USAF*

Opposite below: An air-to-air view of one of the first production B-57Bs which began to reach operational units from the beginning of 1955. Subsequent versions such as the B-57C dual-control trainer and the B-57E target tug were all based on the B-57B airframe.

On 28 June 1954 the first Martin B-57B took to the air. This version was developed as a night intruder bomber and the most obvious change was the redesign of the nose to accommodate the two crew members in tandem under a clear view fighter-type canopy. A fixed armament of eight 0.5in machine guns or four 20mm cannon was installed and underwing hardpoints provided for various combinations of bombs and rockets. The B-52B was the most numerous of the Martin built Canberras with 202 delivered out of a total production of 424 aircraft.

Above: Jack Northrop had long believed in the concept of flying wing designs and in response to a USAAC specification for a long-range strategic bomber he put forward such a project. which was eventually ordered in prototype form as the XB-35. To provide design data and to act as a familiarization trainer for pilots, a one-third scale representative scale model was constructed and the first of four examples flew on 27 December 1942. This was the Northrop N-9M and successfully proved the aerodynamics of the flying wing although the test programme was plagued with engine problems.

Opposite: The first prototype XB-35 was ordered in November 1941 and optimistically the delivery was scheduled for the end of 1943 although the first flight did not actually occur until June 1946. It was powered by four 3,000hp Pratt & Whitney R-4360 radial engines driving contra-rotating propellers but vibration problems led to these being replaced by more conventional single-rotation four-bladed propellers, a change which significantly reduced performance. Despite the potential to offer a better performance than the rival Convair B-36, the two flying prototypes (XB-35 and a single YB-35) were scrapped in 1949 and it is likely that political pressures were a factor in their demise.

Above: Prior to the termination of the XB-35 programme an order had been placed in 1942 for thirteen pre-production YB-35s although only the first of these was flown (May 1948). However, the remaining twelve airframes, most of which are shown in the aerial view of Northrop's airfield at Hawthorn CA, were in an advanced stage of construction and two of these were selected for conversion to jet power as the YB-49. In these aircraft the four R-4360 radial engines were replaced by eight 4,000lb.s.t. Allison J-35 turbojets and the first of these flew on 21 October 1947.

Opposite above: The first XB-49 demonstrated a maximum speed of almost 500mph and a service ceiling in excess of 45,000ft. For its time the XB-49 was an extremely advanced design and although no production orders were forthcoming the experience gained during testing these aircraft was directly applied to the design of the later Northrop Grumman B-2 Stealth Bomber which first flew in 1989 and is in service today. The clear cupola at the rear of the central nacelle was intended to house a gunner who would operate remotely-controlled twin 0.5in machine guns mounted in barbettes above and below the wings.

A close-up view of the jet engine installation on the XB-49. The flying wing design permitted a relatively thick wing in which the engines were completely enclosed, significantly reducing drag. The small fixed vertical fins were necessary to compensate for the loss of keel area caused by the removal of the extended nacelles in the propeller-driven XB-35.

Above: The last chance for Northrop's flying wings was a 1948 contract to convert the tenth XB-35 (42-102376) for the long-range strategic reconnaissance role under the designation YRB-47. There was also a potential contract for a further twenty-nine production RB-49s but it was expected that these would be built by Convair at Fort Worth. The YRB-47 first flew on 4 May 1950 and differed from the earlier YB-49 in that it was powered by only six J-35 turbojets, two of which were mounted in underwing pods. This arrangement made space available in the wing for additional fuel resulting in a 5,000-mile maximum range. However, even before the prototype flew the production contract had been cancelled and the aircraft was used for test and experimental purposes until grounded in 1952.

Opposite above: A fascinating image showing the Northrop XB-49 in formation with a Boeing B-47 Stratojet which gives an indication of the relative size of these two very advanced aircraft.

Opposite below: A flying wing was one of many configurations investigated by Boeing in response to a series of Air Force requirements for a long-range strategic bomber which dated back to 1945. Boeing originally proposed their Model 462, a straight-wing six-turboprop bomber, but subsequently came up with a smaller swept-wing four-turboprop design, the Model 464. This in turn went through several iterations before ending up as the Model 464-67 powered by eight turbojets of which two prototypes were ordered as the XB-52 and YB-52. In fact it was the latter which was the first to fly and is shown here on its maiden flight on 15 April 1952.

Above: An air-to-air view of the YB-52 (49-231) which carries the official name Stratofortress on the nose although this was rarely used. More commonly the big bomber became affectionately known as the 'Buff' (a polite translation being 'Big Ugly Fat Fellow'). Evident in this view is the single canopy covering the pilot and co-pilot who sat in tandem. The navigator and bombardier were housed in the forward fuselage below the pilots and a gunner manned the tail turret which incorporated a radar-directed fire-control system. Both prototypes were powered by eight 8,750lb.s.t. Pratt & Whitney J57 turbojets.

Opposite above: Work on fitting additional equipment delayed the first flight of the XB-52 (49-230) until 2 October 1952. Although the B-52 was similar in outline to the earlier B-47 Stratojet, it was a considerably larger aircraft and its empty weight of 160,000lbs was more than double the 76,000lbs of the latter. Discernible in this view is the slight upward curve of the leading edge of the wings, the tips of which could flex by as much as 20ft in flight.

Opposite below: This close-up ground view of the nose section of XB-52 gives a good idea of the sheer size of this aircraft, especially when set against the Convair B-36 in the background which it would replace in service with SAC. The aircraft in the foreground is the Northrop X-4 Bantam, a tailless research aircraft similar to the British de Havilland DH.108 Swallow. *USAF*

Opposite above: The first production version was the Boeing B-52A which featured a more conventional flight deck allowing the two pilots to sit side by side – a better arrangement for operational flying. They and the flight engineer were provided with upward-firing ejector seats and the navigator and bombardier on the lower deck had downward-ejecting seats – arrangements which were substantially better than those in the contemporary British V-bombers. In the event of an emergency the rear gunner could cause the entire tail turret to be jettisoned before taking to his parachute. Although thirteen B-52As were ordered only three were actually delivered, the first flying on 5 August 1954 and the other two before the end of that year and all were retained by Boeing for development purposes. *USAF*

Opposite below: The first operational version was the B-52B of which a total of fifty were produced (including the RB-52B version) between 1955 and 1957. It was powered by improved versions of the J57 turbojet which could produce up to 12,000lbs.s.t. with water injection. The J57 was one of the first twin-spool turbojets which offered much improved fuel efficiency and, together with wing-mounted auxiliary fuel tanks, endowed the early B-52s with a combat radius of over 3,500 miles which could be increased with in-flight refuelling. Indeed in January 1957, in a demonstration of the global reach of the new bomber, three B-52Bs of the 93rd Bombardment Wing made a non-stop 24,325-mile flight around the world which involved five in-flight refuellings. *USAF*

Above: Amazingly the B-52 is still operational today (2019) no less than sixty-four years after first entering service. The current version is the B-52H, shown here, which is powered by eight 17,000lb.s.t. Pratt & Whitney TF33 turbofans, almost twice the rating of the original J57s. Despite the introduction of later types such as the B-1 Lancer and B-2 Spirit, the B-52 offers an unrivalled combination of range and bomb load (over 70,000lbs of ordnance). Although the last B-52H was delivered in 1962 there are still around seventy still in service and continued refurbishments and upgrades are likely to keep them going for several decades ahead. It is entirely possible that the B-52 could reach the unique milestone of 100 years continuous front-line service – an incredible record. *ASM*

Above: A vital component of SAC was the tanker force which supported the B-47 and B-52 jet bombers. Until the late 1950s this was equipped with the piston-engined KC-97, a tanker version of the C-97 Stratofreighter, although several were converted to KC-97Ls with a pair of underwing J47 turbojets to boost performance. However what was really needed was a jet-powered tanker and following the first flight of Boeing's Model 367-80 prototype on 15 July 1954 the Air Force ordered a tanker version as the KC-135A Stratotanker which subsequently first flew on 31 August 1956. The Model 367-80 (which also formed the basis of the highly successful Boeing 707 airliner) poses here in front of a KC-97 which the jet powered KC-135 would eventually replace.

Opposite above: A potential rival for the Boeing B-52 was the Convair B-60 which was based on the piston-engined B-36, then the principal strategic bomber in service with SAC. In fact the original fuselage was retained but swept tail surfaces were added. A new 35° swept wing was married to the original fuselage attachment points and power was provided by eight 8,700lb.s.t. J57 turbojets mounted in pairs on swept-forward pylons. Two prototypes were ordered in March 1951 and the first of these flew on 18 April 1952, only three days after the YB-52.

Opposite below: The Convair bomber displayed an obvious ancestry from the B-36, as shown in this view at the Fort Worth ramp in 1952. Initially designated as the B-36G, the jet version subsequently became the YB-60 and was of interest to the Air Force as, being based on an existing airframe, it would be quicker and cheaper to produce. *USAF*

Above: Once the YB-60 prototype was flying the Air Force quickly lost interest. It was 100mph slower than the B-52 and displayed severe handling problems which would have been expensive and time-consuming to eradicate. Consequently the programme was cancelled in January 1953 and the second prototype, although structurally complete, did not receive any engines and never flew. Both the prototypes were scrapped in the summer of 1953 and the entire programme had cost over $14 million.

Opposite above: A view of the B-60 cockpit. Although still being fitted out, it shows the complexity of the analogue instrumentation required to monitor the eight engines.

Opposite below: In the immediate post-war era there was intense competition between the US Navy and the USAAF for funds to support an atomic strike capability. While the Air Force lobbied for the long-range B-36 bomber, the Navy proposed a strike aircraft carrying a 10,000lb atomic bomb to be launched from a new carrier (USS *United States*, CV58). In the event the Air Force came out ahead and the carrier was cancelled. However, the Navy had already developed a suitable bomber in the form of the North American AJ Savage which took to the air in prototype form (XAJ-1 shown here) on 3 July 1948. Although basically a piston-engined aircraft (two 2,400hp R-2800 radial engines) its performance was boosted by a J33 jet engine installed in the rear fuselage but when not in use the intake was blanked off by a retractable cover. *AC*

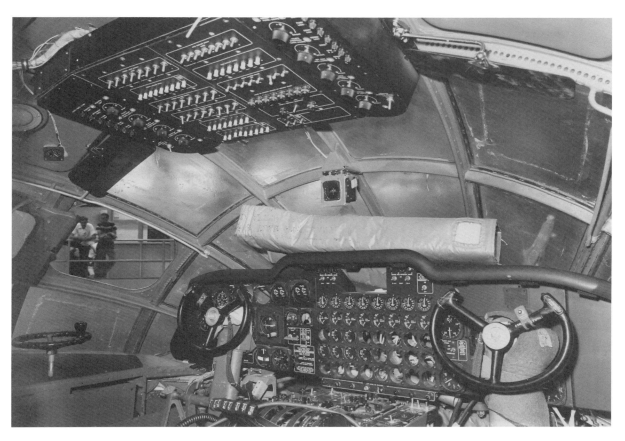

Opposite above: In practice it was found that the Savage could be operated from the existing three *Midway*-class carriers and even from wartime *Essex*-class carriers which had been modernized and upgraded. Here two aircraft of VC-6 Nuclear Attack Squadron prepare to launch from the *Essex*-class carrier USS *Lake Champlain* (CV39) in 1952. Visible in this view is the dorsal intake for the rear-mounted jet engine which was used to boost take-off performance and maximum speed during an attack. As can be seen, the Savage was a large aircraft which posed considerable problems for flight-deck operations. Although the outer wings and tail fin could be folded this was a slow process done manually.

Opposite below: An AJ-1 Savage about launch from USS *Lake Champlain* – note the raised blast screen to deflect the jet exhaust. Maximum speed with the jet booster in operation was 425mph and combat radius carrying a 10,000lb bomb was 1,120 miles. As well as three prototypes, fifty-five AJ-1s were produced followed by eighty-five AJ-2/AJ-2P variants. Becoming operational in 1950 the Savage served in the nuclear strike role until gradually replaced between 1957 and 1959. However, several were converted to act as aerial tankers and continued in that role in the early 1960s.

Above: In an attempt to boost performance, North American produced the turboprop-powered XA2J-1 Super Savage. Although development began in 1948, the prototype did not fly until 4 January 1952. The delay was due to problems with the 5,000shp Allison T40 turboprops, each of which was basically a pair of T38 turboprops driving large contra-rotating propellers through a combined gearbox. The rear fuselage jet engine was deleted and maximum speed was estimated at 450mph. However the protracted development meant that much faster jet attack aircraft were now in prospect and the Super Savage programme was cancelled. *WC*

Above: The successor to the AJ Savage in the nuclear strike role was the Douglas A3D Skywarrior and the prototype XA3D-1 (125412 shown here) flew on 28 October 1952. The Skywarrior was an exceptionally clean design by Ed Heinemann (who also designed the A4D Skyhawk) and was powered by two 7,000lb.s.t. Westinghouse J40-WE-3 engines in pylon-mounted underwing pods. A crew of three was carried, maximum bomb load was 12,000lbs and a pair of radar-directed 20mm cannon were mounted in the tail.

Opposite above: The A3D was one of many naval projects of the era which depended on the J40 engine which turned out to be a total failure and development was cancelled. Fortunately it was relatively easy to redesign the engine mountings and nacelles to accept an alternative power plant in the form of the more powerful 9,700lb.s.t. Pratt & Whitney J57 turbojet. The first J57 variant flew in September 1953 but other development issues delayed the Skywarrior's entry into operational service until the spring of 1956.

Opposite below: The initial Skywarrior was the A3D-1, of which fifty were delivered, but the main production variant was the A3D-2 (230 of all versions produced), deliveries of which began in 1957 and one of which is shown here in the grey/white camouflage scheme adopted by the US Navy from 1955 onwards. The Skywarrior squadrons maintained the US Navy's nuclear strike capability until 1964 when the first Polaris-equipped nuclear submarines entered service. However, many continued in service in other roles including reconnaissance, aerial refuelling and electronic warfare and the last operational example was not retired until 1991.

Above: At the outbreak of the Korean War in 1950 the standard USAF light bomber was the B-26 Invader and it was soon apparent that a jet-powered replacement was urgently required. In an unusual move the Air Force decided that the Navy's A3D Skywarrior then under development could provide the basis for a new tactical bomber which could become quickly available. Initially it was intended that only minimal modifications would be made including the deletion of naval features such as folding wings, arrester hook and strengthened undercarriage. However, different engines, a revised wing and other changes resulted in an almost new aircraft although it retained the basic shape and configuration of the A3D. Consequently the first of five pre-production RB-66A Destroyers (52-2830 shown here) did not fly until 28 June 1954. *USAF*

Opposite above: The RB-66A was powered by a pair of 9,750lb.s.t. Allison J71 turbojets replacing the J57s in the naval A3D. It was also manned by a crew of three but, unlike the Navy jet, they were all provided with upward-firing ejector seats. A total of 293 Destroyers was produced, most of which were the camera equipped RB-66, but there were also 72 B-66B bombers which could carry up to 15,000lbs of bombs (53-480 shown here was the penultimate production example) and both variants entered operational service in 1956. The later RB-66C was equipped for the ECM role and by the time of the Vietnam War many of the earlier aircraft were converted for the same purpose as the EB-66. The last Destroyer was retired from USAF service in 1975.

Opposite below: As early as 1949 the Air Force was looking ahead to the possibility of a supersonic bomber and following various design and feasibility studies a contract was awarded to Convair in April 1952. The result was the Convair XB-58 which eventually flew on 11 November 1956 and consequently really lies outside the period covered by this book but it does give an indication of the future of the bomber as seen at that time. Intended to operate at high speeds and altitudes, the Hustler was forced to operate at low altitudes and subsonic speeds due to the improvement in Soviet surface-to-air missiles. Consequently any advantage in supersonic performance was lost and so the B-58 only had a relatively brief career operational career from 1960 to 1970 when it was retired, outlived by the various types it was expected to replace.

Chapter 5

The Soviet Union

Before and during the Second World War, there was a tendency amongst Western air forces to regard Soviet aircraft as technically inferior to their own and this attitude persisted until well into the Cold War era. Initially this may have had some substance given the poor performance of Soviet-supplied Republican fighters against the Nationalist Messerschmitt Bf 109 fighters and Heinkel He 111 bombers in the Spanish Civil War while in 1941 the German Luftwaffe easily brushed aside the Soviet opposition. It wasn't until around 1943 that the mass production of improved types by the Soviet aircraft factories began to turn the tide and even then the emphasis was on quantity rather than quality.

When German forces invaded Soviet Russia in June 1941 the only four-engined long-range bomber available to the Soviet Air Force was the Petlyakov Pe-8. However, it was only produced in small numbers (ninety-three in total) and its operational use was extremely limited. Powered by four 1,350hp AM-35A V-12 engines, it had a maximum speed of 275mph and a range of up to 2,250 miles although this was reduced when carrying the maximum 8,000lb bomb load. *NARA*

The Soviet Air Force (VVS) was almost entirely structured to support the Army and consequently concentrated on light bombers and attack aircraft. The only four-engined heavy bomber available in 1941 was the Petlyakov Pe-8 which had flown in prototype form (as the TB-7) in 1936. Production was terminated in 1941 in favour of the twin-engined Pe-2 light bomber which was one of the outstandingly successful Soviet aircraft of the time, with over 11,000 examples produced. The Tupolev Tu-2 medium bomber, first flown in 1941, was another successful design and both these types stood comparison with contemporary Western aircraft.

By 1945 the VVS had formulated the need for a strategic bomber and this was met by producing a reverse-engineered copy of the American B-29 Superfortress, three examples of which had made forced landings in Soviet territory in 1944–5. This became the Tupolev Tu-4 which went on to form the backbone of the Soviet bomber force until the advent of jet bombers in the 1950s. The design and development of jet-propelled bombers was facilitated by the occupation of eastern Germany in 1945 when many factories producing jet engines and aircraft were overrun. The Soviets were quick to adopt and adapt German technology and

The VVS was much like the German Luftwaffe, which also failed to develop a long-range strategic bomber, in that its operational priority was to act in support of ground operations by the Army. For this it required various light bombers and ground-attack aircraft but almost all were types which were in service or under development in 1941. The only new light bomber to be developed during the war was the Tupolev Tu-2 which was fast (340mph) and could carry up to 8,800lbs of bombs in an internal bomb bay supplemented by two underwing hardpoints. Only around 1,100 had been delivered by the end of the war but total production reached 2,527 and the type saw widespread use in the immediate post-war era before being retired from VVS service in 1950.

In late 1944 three American B-29 Superfortress bombers force landed in Soviet Far Eastern territory and although the crews were repatriated, the aircraft were retained and used as patterns for the reverse-engineering process which resulted in the Tupolev Tu-4. The first of these only flew on 19 May 1947, the timescale due to the enormous effort involved in checking over 100,000 separate items to confirm material specifications and dimensions (converted to metric units) so that they could be reproduced. This process involved not only the engines and airframe, but also systems such as electrics, hydraulics, navigation and defensive armament.

captured Jumo 004 and BMW 003 jet engines were used to power various Soviet prototypes. In terms of jet-engine technology the biggest post-war boost came from Britain where the Labour government authorized the export of Rolls-Royce Nene and Derwent jet engines to Russia. These were also reverse-engineered as the RD-45 and RD500, and were used to power a range of military aircraft including some of the early jet bombers.

The Soviet aircraft industry had been nationalized as far back as 1918 and under the Stalinist regime it was tightly controlled. Indeed, at various times several of the leading aircraft designers such as Andrei Tupolev and Vladimir Petlyakov were arrested, although they were allowed to work at design bureaus established within the gulag system. Unlike Western aircraft manufacturers, aircraft designers worked with a team at their own design bureau (OKB) but subsequent manufacture would be allocated to one or more state owned factories (GAZ). In the post-war era bombers were almost exclusively designed by the Ilyushin and Tupolev bureaus.

An impressive line-up of Soviet-built Tu-4 bombers. One significant change incorporated in these aircraft compared to the American original was that the 0.5in machine guns in the remotely-controlled barbettes and the manned tail turret were replaced by harder-hitting 23mm cannon. Over 800 Tu-4s were delivered between 1947 and 1951 and they continued in VVS service until replaced by the jet-powered Tu-16 from 1954 onwards. Subsequently some surplus Tu-4s were exported to China. Tupolev produced substantially developed versions as the Tu-80 and Tu-85 which were flown in prototype form but the projected turboprop-powered Tu-94 was never built.

Many early Soviet jet bombers such as the Ilyushin Il-22 were clearly based on German designs, while others such as the Tupolev Tu-77 were produced by modifying an existing type and replacing the original piston engines with jet units. However, it was not long before the Soviet bureaux were producing bombers of their own design powered by domestically-developed engines which were as good as, if not better than, their Western equivalents. Types such as the Ilyushin Il-28, which first flew in 1948, and the Tupolev Tu-16 (1952) were produced in great numbers and exported to many air forces within the Soviet sphere of influence. A unique achievement was the production of the massive Tu-95

'Bear' long-range strategic bomber which first flew in 1954 and remains the only successful bomber powered by turboprops. By the mid-1950s advanced supersonic bombers such as the Tu-22M and Myasishchyev M-50 were on the drawing boards and by that time Soviet military aircraft were in no way inferior to their Western counterparts.

Soviet aircraft type designations were often confusing. Before 1940 new types were allocated a design number in sequence with a prefix indicating role (notably I for fighter and B for bomber, an example being the Polikarpov I-15). After that date the design bureau's identification letters were followed again by sequential numbers except that fighters were allocated odd numbers (e.g. Yak-9, MiG-15) and bombers given even numbers (e.g. Tu-2, Pe-8). However, fighters at least continued to be known initially by their I number (e.g. the MiG-15 was originally the I-310). Another confusing element was that aircraft might be developed under the bureau designation which would change to a VVS designation when the type was accepted for service. So, for example, the Tupolev Tu-72 became the better-known Tu-14. In 1947 the USAF adopted its own system, giving each identified aircraft a Type number so that Type 1 was the MiG-9, Type 2 the Yak-15 and so on, although there was no logic to the number sequence. In an effort to resolve this confusion NATO and other allied countries adopted a simple code name for each type with the initial letter indicating the role (e.g. F – Fighter, B – Bomber, C – Cargo etc). The following is a list of the code names relevant to the types described in this chapter.

Ilyushin Il-28	'Beagle'
Ilyushin Il-54	'Blowlamp'
Myasishchyev M-4	'Bison'
Tupolev Tu-2	'Bat'
Tupolev Tu-14	'Bosun'
Tupolev Tu-16	'Badger'
Tupolev Tu-95	'Bear'
Yakovlev Yak-28B	'Brewer'

Note: Unless otherwise credited, all the images in this chapter are sourced from the Russian Aircraft Research Trust.

Andrei Nikolayevich Tupolev was perhaps the world's most prolific aircraft designer, although many of his later types were actually produced by others under his direction. Born in 1888, among his many early achievements were the first Russian all-metal aircraft (ANT-1) and the massive ANT-6 four-engined monoplane bomber which first flew in 1930. In 1937 he was arrested in a Stalinist purge and set to work in a gulag-based OKB. However, his success in producing the Tu-2 light bomber resulted in his release in 1943 and he quickly became involved in the design and production of a series of successful jet bombers, as well as the Tu-104 and later jet airliners. This photo was taken in 1968 on the occasion of his 80th birthday.

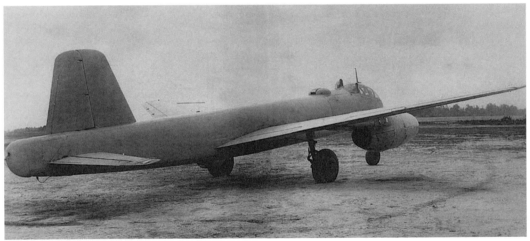

The Junkers team relocated to the Soviet Union in 1946 and as the OKB 1 design bureau was tasked with continuing work on several jet designs which had been under development at the end of the war. One of these was the EF-140 shown here and while the nose and fuselage was clearly based on the wartime Ju 388, this was mated to the revolutionary swept-forward wings and was powered by two Mikulin AM-TKRD-01 turbojets in underwing nacelles. The Soviet-built prototype flew on 30 September 1948 and during testing demonstrated a maximum speed of 561mph and a range of 1,250 miles.

Above: The EF-140 was redesigned as the 140-R which was of similar configuration but smaller and featured wingtip fuel tanks. Powered by Klimov VK-1 turbojets derived from the Rolls-Royce Nene it was intended for the reconnaissance role and made the first of only four flights on 12 October 1949. A second prototype intended for the dual bomber/reconnaissance role was almost complete when the whole programme, including the EF-140, was terminated in July 1950.

Opposite above: The Junkers team, headed by Dr Bruno Baade, also worked on the EF-150 which was a slightly more conventional design with swept-back shoulder-mounted wings and a pair of pod-mounted Lyulka 10,100lb.s.t. TR-3/AL-5 axial-flow turbojets. With a loaded weight of around 119,000lbs (54,000kg) it was larger than the EF-140 and was armed with a remote-controlled dorsal turret and a manned rear turret, both mounting twin 23mm cannon. A 13,230lb (6000kg) bomb load could be carried.

Opposite below: In some respects the EF150 was similar to the American B-47 Stratojet with its pylon-mounted engines, swept wing and tandem undercarriage. Notable in this overhead view are the wingtip nacelles housing the outrigger wheels and the prominent wing fences.

Opposite above: The EF-150 (sometimes referred to as the Samolet 150) introduced a number of advanced features including the tandem main wheel undercarriage with wingtip-mounted outriggers. Not immediately obvious is that the aerodynamic surfaces (ailerons, elevators etc.) were actuated by electrical mechanisms making this a very early example of 'fly-by-wire'. Only a single prototype was completed which flew on 9 May 1952 after delays due to bureaucratic issues which gave the German OKB team a low priority.

Opposite below: The first Soviet-designed jet bomber was the Ilyushin Il-22 which took to the air on 24 July 1947. In overall configuration (a straight shoulder-mounted wing with four jet engines in separate nacelles) it was remarkably similar to the German Arado Ar 234 V6 but was a considerably larger and heavier aircraft. The main undercarriage units retracted into the fuselage which also featured an internal bomb bay capable of carrying up to 4,400lbs of bombs. Although the prototype performed satisfactorily, no production orders were forthcoming.

Above: This official model of the Il-22 clearly illustrates the layout of this pioneering aircraft which was also notable in that the Lyulka TR-1 engines were of entirely Soviet design. Arkhip Mikhailovich Lyulka began development of an axial-flow jet engine as early as 1938 and by 1944 had the TR-1 with an eight-stage compressor running at 2,860lb.s.t. This was considerably more powerful than the contemporary German Jumo 004B and early British Rolls-Royce Derwent engines.

ILIUCHIN-DESIGNED
Experimental Soviet 4–Jet Bomber.

Above: An American intelligence appreciation of the II-22 in 1948 following its appearance at the 1947 Tushino military display. In essence it is remarkably accurate, the main mistake being to show the engines as being pylon-mounted instead of directly attached below the wing. An interesting feature was the inclusion of an Ilyushin-designed pressurized tail turret, something which became standard on virtually all Soviet jet bombers. There was also a remotely-controlled dorsal barbette with twin 23mm cannon. The II-22 had a maximum speed of 446mph and a service ceiling of just under 40,000ft.

Opposite above: On 27 July 1947, only three days after the II-22 had flown, another Soviet jet bomber took to the skies. This had the OKB designation Tupolev Tu-77 but was later given the VVS designation Tu-12. In an effort to get a jet bomber flying, Tupolev took the basic Tu-2 design and substituted a pair of jet engines for the original radial piston engines. Other changes included the adoption of a tricycle undercarriage and a re-arrangement of the crew layout in the fuselage which was unpressurized. The internal bomb bay could take up to 6,600lbs of bombs.

Opposite below: The prototype was actually powered by British Rolls-Royce Nene engines from a batch which Rolls-Royce had been permitted to export to the Soviet Union. It was followed by a further five production aircraft and all eventually received Klimov RD45 engines which were Soviet-made exact copies of the Nene. The Tu-12 had a defensive armament of two 12.7mm machine guns in rearward-firing dorsal and ventral positions plus a fixed forward-firing 23mm cannon. Although not allocated to a front-line unit, the Tu-12 was used to give pilots and crews jet experience and also in trials with jet fighters such as the MiG-9 to evolve suitable tactics for jet-age combat.

Above: Even while producing the Tu-12, Tupolev was looking at a more advanced jet bomber intended for the Soviet Naval Aviation. This was the Tu-72 which would be powered by a pair of Rolls-Royce Nene engines and featured a capacious bomb bay capable of carrying mines and/or torpedoes. However, at an early stage it was realized that the aircraft would be underpowered and it was redesigned as the Tu-73 with a tail-mounted Rolls-Royce Derwent engine as a booster for take-off and for high-speed dashes during an attack. On the first prototype, which flew on 24 October 1947, a retractable fairing covered the dorsal intake for the tail-mounted jet engine.

Opposite above: The second Tu-73 was flown on 20 December 1947 and had a conventional fixed rear intake. It also carried the proposed defensive armament of remotely-controlled dorsal and ventral barbettes mounting twin 23mm cannon. It was intended that the aircraft would enter production under the military designation Tu-14 and this logo is painted on the nose and tail. In this form the maximum loaded weight was 24.2 tonnes (53,350lbs) and expected maximum speed was 542mph.

Opposite below: A rear view of the Tu-73 showing the three-engine layout. Other points of interest are the four PSR-1500-15 rocket boosters (under the wing centre section) for improved take-off performance and the Plexiglas bulged panels on either side of the fuselage. The latter provided a field of view for the gunner who operated the ventral PS23 turret.

Opposite above: The third prototype, flown on 7 May 1948, featured some minor changes and for OKB purposes was designated Tu-78 although it still carries the Tu-14 logo. The main difference was that it was powered by Soviet-built RD45 and RD500 engines, copies of the Rolls-Royce Nene and Derwent respectively, and the retractable fairing again covered the dorsal intake. Other changes included increased fuel tankage and a slight increase in fuselage length. The only obvious external difference was that the navigator's side windows in the nose had a rectangular instead of round profile.

Opposite below: Although the British Nene engine was copied as the RD45, engineer Vladimir Klimov made intensive efforts to improve the design and this resulted in the VK-1 which raised the thrust rating to 5,950lb.s.t. – almost 20 per cent more than the original Nene. Tupolev realized that this increased power enabled him to do away with the third engine in the tail and the result was the twin-engined (VK-1) Tupolev Tu-81. Subsequently tail and dorsal remotely-controlled barbettes were deleted and replaced by a manned tail turret with a pair of 23mm cannon. In this form the aircraft flew as the Tu-14 in October 1949. Capable of carrying up to 6,600lbs (3,000kg) of bombs, it had a maximum speed of 497mph at sea level.

Above: The Tu-14 had been designed to meet VVF requirements for a tactical bomber but lost out to the Ilyushin Il-28 (q.v.). However it was evaluated by the Soviet Navy as a high-speed torpedo bomber and in this role was ordered into production as the Tu-14T, although only eighty-nine aircraft were eventually delivered (including a single Tu-14R reconnaissance version). This side view shows the final production version which featured a cutaway rudder and an improved tail turret, and could carry two torpedoes. The Soviet Navy regarded these fast jet torpedo bombers as a way of countering the US Navy's carrier fleet.

Another modification incorporated in production Tu-14s was the provision of a downward-firing ejector seat for the tail gunner although this was of limited use at low altitudes. This interesting sequence shows the system being tested.

One of the most successful of the early post-war Soviet jet bombers was the twin-engined Ilyushin Il-28. Very similar in concept to the rival Tupolev Tu-14, it was also powered by a pair of Nene-derived engines but was lighter and had a shorter fuselage. Performance was similar although it was faster at altitude and it could also carry up to 6,600lbs (3,000kg) of bombs or torpedoes. The prototype, powered by a pair of Rolls-Royce Nene engines, flew on 8 August 1948. A second prototype powered by Russian built RD-45 engines flew before the end of the year.

On paper there was little to choose between the two rival designs so the head of the Air Force, Marshal Vershinin, ordered that three regular VVF crews, chosen at random, should test both. These unanimously favoured the Ilyushin Il-28, manly on the grounds of its easier handling and better manoeuvrability. On Stalin's orders twenty-five production examples were delivered to the VVF in time to take part in the 1950 May Day flypasts and subsequently the Il-28 saw widespread service with the Soviet Air Force with over 2,000 being built, many remaining in service until the early 1980s.

A tail gunner prepares to access the Ilyushin bomber's pressurized Il-K6 tail turret via the ventral hatch. The guns were a pair of Nudelman-Rikhter NR-23 cannon each capable of firing up to 950 rounds per minute, an incredibly high rate of fire. Contemporary fighters were not much faster than the new jet bombers so most interceptions ended up as a drawn-out tail chase giving the defensive tail guns a good chance of fighting off the attacker, especially when radar-directed fire-control systems were later fitted. This situation eventually led to the evolution of collision-course interception tactics by jet fighters.

The Il-28 was produced in several specialized versions. This is the Il-28T torpedo bomber which was ordered by the Soviet Navy where it eventually replaced the Tu-14T. In this instance it shows the wingtip fuel tanks that were also sometimes carried by other variants. Some later Il-28s converted for EW roles adapted the tanks as housing for various antennas.

At a very early stage a two-seat trainer, the Il-28U, was produced and used to train pilots for the 1950 May Day parade. The trainee pilot sat in under the standard bubble canopy while the nose was redesigned to provide a station for the instructor whose controls could override the trainee's if necessary. The tail armament was deleted but the position was occupied by a radio operator.

Over 1,100 Il-28s were exported to air forces within the Soviet sphere of influence. This is one of four Il-28s modified as target tugs and supplied to Finland in the early 1960s. More significantly, large numbers of bomber versions were supplied to other nations including Egypt, Hungary, Romania, North Korea and China. The type was actually produced under licence in Czechoslovakia as the Avia B-228 and built in China as the Harbin H-5, of which approximately 2,000 were built for domestic use and export, although this was an unlicensed version.

A 1948 specification called for a jet bomber capable of carrying a 2,000kg bomb load over a distance of 3,500km at a speed of 1,000km/h (621mph). The Ilyushin OKB drew up the Il-30 design loosely based on the Il-28 but featuring wings swept at 35° and powered by a pair of Lyulka TR-3 axial flow turbojets rated at 10,000lb.s.t. A tandem undercarriage was adopted, the first on any Soviet aircraft and the sole prototype flew on 9 September 1949. (The EF150 described earlier did not fly untill 1952.)

Apart from the previous image, photographs of the Il-30 are extremely rare (if not non-existent) but this view of a contemporary model illustrates the major features of the design. Defensive armament comprised six NR-23 cannon in remotely-control dorsal and ventral barbettes and a manned tail turret. Although the target speed of 1,000km/h was achieved, in other aspects it was less than satisfactory. It was almost twice as heavy as the Il-28 and the swept wing produced serious handling deficiencies which were only partly mitigated by the eight full chord wing fences eventually fitted. Consequently no production orders were forthcoming.

In the late 1940s the VVF was already looking ahead for a jet replacement for the Tu-4 copy of the Superfortress and a specification was issued requiring an aircraft able to carry a 5,000kg bomb load over a range of 5,000km (3,105 miles). Initially the Ilyushin OKB considered an enlarged Il-30 as a basis but potential problems with the strength requirements of the swept wing and fuel/CG issues led to a straight wing being adopted. The resulting Ilyushin Il-46 was then in effect a much enlarged Il-28 but with substantially more power available in the form of two 10,000lb.s.t. Lyulka AL-5 turbojets. Maximum loaded weight was in the region of 92,000lbs (42,000kg) and a much stronger undercarriage was required in which the twin main wheel units were actually carried on separate legs, one retracting forwards and the other rearwards into the engine nacelle.

Above: The sole prototype Il-46 flew on 3 March 1952 and was thus a contemporary of the British Valiant and Vulcan, and the American B-52. It could carry a bomb load of up to 13,250lbs (6,000kg) at speeds up to 577mph (928km/h) although the 5,000km (3,105-mile) range was only possible with a reduced bomb load. Reputedly the aircraft handled well but single-engine performance was barely acceptable and the Tu-4 replacement contract was eventually won by a Tupolev design.

Opposite above: The last jet bomber designed by the Ilyushin OKB was the Il-54 which resulted from a 1952 VVS specification for a supersonic tactical bomber capable of Mach 1.15 with a 6,000kg (13,200lb) bomb load. After investigating various configurations a 55° swept wing was adopted and the power plants were pair of 14,330lb.s.t. (up to 19,800lb.s.t. with afterburning) Lyulka AL-7. The tandem undercarriage design posed some problems as the sharply-swept wing required a high angle of attack on take-off to generate the necessary lift and to achieve this a pilot-operated mechanism extended the nose wheel leg to increase AoA from the static setting of 5°45' to 10° at the point of lift off. Also the long wheelbase necessitated by the size of the bomb bay meant that the fuselage centre section had to be considerably strengthened to take the bending loads and this added to the aircraft's structural weight.

Opposite below: Again, photos of an Ilyushin prototype are scarce but this view of a contemporary model clearly shows the sharp sweepback applied to the wing and tail surfaces. Although completed in June 1954, the first flight did not occur until 3 April 1955. In 1956 it was revealed to Western observers who mistakenly assumed that it was in service with the VVF and consequently allocated it the NATO code name 'Blowlamp'. In fact only the one prototype was ever completed although plans existed for trainer (Il-54U) and torpedo bomber (Il-54T) versions. Thereafter the Ilyushin OKB concentrated successfully on the design and production of jet and turboprop airliners and transports.

Opposite above: The first swept-wing Russian bomber to fly was the Tupolev Tu-82 which took to the air on 24 March 1949. It was based on the Tu-14 but featured a 35° swept wing and tail surfaces and was powered by a pair of Mikulin VK-1 turbojets. The armament was similar (two fixed forward-firing cannon and twin cannon in dorsal and tail positions). The cross section of the fuselage was oval rather than round and the Tu-82 was actually slightly smaller and lighter than the Tu-14.

Opposite below: The swept wing on the Tu-82 also featured some anhedral (a common arrangement on aircraft with shoulder-mounted swept wings) to assist stability and this required that the nose wheel leg be lengthened to achieve the required angle of attack on take-off. The main wheels, retracting into the engine nacelles were identical to those on the Tu-14.

Above: This rear view of the Tu-82 emphasizes the depth of the oval-section fuselage. Provision was made for mounting a pair of B-20e 20mm cannon but these were never installed in the sole prototype and work on the design was subsequently halted in favour of the more promising Tu-88. Interestingly the service designation for the Tu-82 was Tu-22 (appropriate logos on nose and tail) but this subsequently allocated to the supersonic Tu-105 which flew in 1958.

Above: Tupolev's answer to the requirement for a jet-powered successor to the Tu-4/B-29 was the Tu-88, a large twin jet with swept wings and tail surfaces and with the engines mounted at the wing roots. Compared to the rival Il-46 it was a much more advanced aircraft and the prototype first flew on 27 April 1952. Following successful trials it was ordered into production as the Tu-16 in December 1952 and the first examples entered service in early 1954. Eventually over 1,500 Tu-16s were delivered from Soviet factories before production ceased in the early 1960s and subsequently many were rebuilt for conversion to various specialized roles.

Opposite above: The first production batches were either Tu-16s for the conventional bombing role or the Tu-16A, modified for carrying nuclear weapons (NATO code name 'Badger A'). At the same time the AV-MF had ordered a maritime version as the Tu-16KS ('Badger B', shown here) which could carry two KS-1 long-range anti-ship missiles on the underwing pylons visible in this photo. The first of these flew in August 1954 and subsequently over 100 were built including 25 for Indonesia. The prospect of mass attacks by missile-carrying Tu-16s was something which caused considerable concern to the US Navy and its carrier fleet.

Opposite below: A later version optimized for the anti-shipping role was the Tu-16K-10 ('Badger C') although this did not fly until 1958 and only entered service in the early 1960s. The distinguishing feature was the revised nose with a prominent radome covering the antenna for a YeN search and tracking radar for use in conjunction with a 200-mile range AS-2 ('Kipper') cruise missile recessed into the bomb bay. This view illustrates the general configuration of the Tu-16 with the engines slightly recessed into the fuselage sides and the intakes and exhausts canted slightly outwards. Noteworthy are the prominent wing fences and the streamlined fairings for the main undercarriage units. *USN via RART*

This side view of an AV-MF Tu-16 illustrates the length of the slim fuselage while the measuring pole gives an indication of the size of this elegant bomber, roughly 9.5m (31.7ft) to the top of the fuselage behind the flight deck. The standard Tu-16 had a maximum loaded weight of around 75 tonnes (165,350lbs) and was powered by a pair of RD-3M turbojets initially rated at just over 19,000lb.s.t. but increased in later versions to 21,000lb.s.t. Thus the total power available was similar to that produced by the four Rolls-Royce Avons in the contemporary British Vickers Valiant and the two aircraft were very comparable in terms of weights and performance.

Crews of a regiment equipped with the Tu-16KS parade in front of their aircraft which are each armed with a pair of KS-1 Komet (NATO code name 'Kennel') anti-ship missiles which had a range of 50–60 miles and were powered by RD-500 engines (a Soviet copy of the Rolls-Royce Derwent).

In common with other Soviet jet bombers of the period, the Tu-16 carried a tail turret for defensive purposes, in this case mounting a pair of long-barrelled AM-23 23mm cannon capable of 1,100 rounds per minute. Recessed remotely-controlled dorsal and ventral turrets each carried a pair of short-barrelled AM-23s and a single fixed nose-mounted AM-23 was operated by the pilot.

Above: The Tu-16 was widely exported and was built under licence in China as the H-6. This example is in the colours of the Egyptian Air Force which only retired its last one in 2000. Over 1,500 Tu-16s were produced in Soviet factories and the type remained in front-line service with the navy and air force until the mid-1990s. Over 100 were produced in China, some of which were exported to Egypt and Iraq.

Opposite above: In the later stages of the bomber's career several aircraft were modified as the Tu-16LL to act as test beds for new jet engines under development. These were generally installed in a separate nacelle which was recessed into the weapons bay but could be lowered into an undisturbed airstream in flight. This example carries a Kuznetzov NK-6 turbofan which was rated at around 44,000lb.s.t and was designed for supersonic flight.

Opposite below: The Tu-16 bomber provided the basis for the Tupolev Tu-104 jet airliner which, with minor modifications, utilized the bomber's wings, tail surfaces and undercarriage units mated to a new wide fuselage initially accommodating up to 50 passengers (increased to over 100 in later versions). The prototype flew in June 1955 and regular services began the following year. Although uneconomic to operate in Western terms, the Tu-104 can be regarded as the world's first successful jet airliner bearing in mind the catastrophes which blighted the early career of the British Comet. *NARA*

Opposite above: Tupolev's great masterpiece was the turboprop Tu-95, better known by its very appropriate NATO code name 'Bear'. It had its origins in a requirement for a bomber capable of carrying an 11,000lb bomb load at 560mph for a range of 7,450 miles. Like the contemporary Boeing B-52, the Tupolev OKB considered several design variations including a swept-wing bomber powered by six turbojets. However, the better range characteristics of turboprops led to their adoption in the final Tu-95 design and the prototype Tu-95/1 flew 12 November 1952. However, a second prototype, the Tu-95/2 shown here, did not fly until February 1955 and the first true production model, shown here was completed in August of that year.

Opposite below: The original Tu-95/1 was powered by eight Kuznetzov 6,000hp TV-2 turboprops arranged in pairs driving four sets of AV-60N contra-rotating propellers. Unfortunately it (and the crew) were lost in an accident in May 1953 when a gearbox failure caused an engine to break up. In the meantime work had already commenced on the Tu-95/2 which would be powered by four 12,000hp TV-13 turboprops, again driving contra-rotating propellers. The airframe was complete by mid-1954 but delays with the engine development meant that it did not fly until 16 February 1955. The size and complexity of the Tu-95 and its power plants is evident in this view of engineers working on the aircraft.

Above: Following on from the initial batch of Tu-95s and Tu-95As was the Tu-95M which had more powerful 15,000hp NK-12M engines, an increased take-off weight (182 tonnes) and fuel capacity. This resulted in an unrefuelled range of 8,200 miles, considerably more than the rival jet-powered B-52 although its cruising speed was some 60mph (100km/hr) slower. The Tu-95M, which entered service in 1957 served as a basis for subsequent variants optimized for reconnaissance, anti-ship strike, over-the-horizon targeting and cruise missile launching. It also formed the basis of the Tu-142, a specialized ASW aircraft which first flew in 1968.

Above: Like the B-52, many examples of the Tu-95 and Tu-142 remain in service today performing front-line operational tasks and seem likely to do so for many years yet. During the type's over 60-year career to date, it has often been seen over the world's oceans or testing the defences of Western nations' sovereign airspace. In such situations the interceptor concerned is often photographed alongside the Soviet bomber, typical example being this RAF Lightning F.6 of Leuchars-based 23 Squadron escorting a Tu-95RT ('Bear-D') over the North Sea in 1966. *MoD via RART*

Opposite above: A potential rival to the Tu-95 was the Myasishchev M-4 (NATO code name 'Bison') whose development was also prompted by intelligence concerning the American B-52 project and design work began in 1949, although the prototype did not fly until 20 January 1953. The M-4 was clean design with a high aspect-ratio wing swept at 34°48' except for the inboard third which where it increased to 37°30'. Power was provided by four 21,000lb.s.t. Mikulin AM-3D turbojets mounted in pairs at the wing roots. A tandem main wheel undercarriage was adopted, supplemented by wingtip outrigger wheels. The original defensive armament comprised no less than ten 23mm cannon in remotely-controlled dorsal and ventral barbettes and a manned tail turret although this was subsequently reduced as a weight-saving measure.

Opposite below: Western air forces only became aware of the existence of the M-4 when the prototype, escorted by MiG-17 fighters, appeared at the 1954 May Day flypast. Subsequently several appeared in formation the following year although in fact only a relatively small number (ninety-three including prototypes) were ever produced. This was mainly because the initial M-4 variants were sadly deficient in range and this resulted in an improved M-6 variant (also known as the 3M/'Bison B') which first flew in March 1956. More powerful VD-7 engines enabled increased fuel capacity to give an unrefuelled range of 7,500 miles with a 5-tonne bomb load. Even so, most M4s/M-6s were converted as aerial tankers or maritime patrol aircraft and were rarely employed in the strategic bombing role.

Above: Apart from the Myasishchev M-4, the production of Soviet jet bombers was the exclusive preserve of the Ilyushin and Tupolev OKBs. However, in June 1952 a twin-engined jet fighter originating from the Yakovlev OKB made its first flight. Its original bureau designation was Yak-120 but it became better known as the Yak-25 (NATO code name 'Flashlight') in PVO service. In many respects it was similar in size and configuration to the contemporary French Vautour and, like that aircraft, it was produced in many variants. As well as a radar-equipped all-weather fighter (entering service in 1955) there were also attack and reconnaissance versions and a single prototype bomber (Yak-123)

Opposite above: The Yak-125B was another bomber prototype based on the Yak-25 airframe. Apart from the inclusion of a navigator/bomb aimer station in the glazed nose, the forward unit of the tandem main undercarriage was moved forward to allow room behind for a radome housing the antenna for an RMM-2 navigation and bomb aiming radar. A twin nose wheel replaced the single wheel of the fighter variant to cater for the increased all up weight. The Yak-125B was intended as a tactical nuclear bomber and was first flown in late 1954. However, after completing a test programme in 1955 the project was terminated in favour of a supersonic tactical bomber then also under development by the Yakovlev OKB.

Below: The Yak-25 and its many derivatives were powered by versions of the Mikulin AM-5 turbojet, initially rated at 4,190lb.s.t. but raised to 4,750lbs (5,952lbs with afterburning) in later versions. The availability of the more powerful AM-9 (redesignated RD-9 from 1956) offering in excess of 6,000lb.s.t. and specifically designed for supersonic flight resulted in the Yak-26 which first flew in the summer of 1955. Compared to the Yak-125B the wing was thinner and more sharply swept, a sharper nose profile was adopted and the engines were housed in lengthened nacelles. Capable of Mach 1.32 at 35,000ft, the Yak-26 was the world's first supersonic light tactical bomber. However, only a small production batch of ten aircraft was built as once again the Yakovlev OKB was in the process of producing something even more advanced.

The ultimate product of the Yakovlev line of twin-engined fighters and bombers was the Yak-28 of which the first prototype illustrated here flew on 5 March 1958. This puts it outside the scope of this book but is included here to complete the story. Powered by a pair of Tumanskii R-11 turbojets, developed versions of which eventually produced over 13,000lb.s.t. with afterburning, the Yak-28B was capable of Mach 1.79 at high altitude. The Yak-28 (NATO code name 'Brewer') was produced in quantity as a reconnaissance aircraft and interceptor as well as a bomber and remained in front-line service until the early 1990s.

Selected Bibliography

Alexander, Jean, *Russian Aircraft since 1940* (Putnam Aeronautical Books, 1975)

Barnes, C.H., *Handley Page Aircraft since 1907* (Putnam Aeronautical Books, 2nd edition, 1987)

Barnes, C.H., *Shorts Aircraft since 1900* (Putnam Aeronautical Books, 2nd edition, 1999)

Brookes, Andrew, *V-Force, The History of Britain's Airborne Deterrent* (Jane's Publishing Co., 1982)

Francillon, Réne J., *McDonnell Douglas Aircraft since 1920* (2 vols) (Putnam Aeronautical Books, 1988)

Gunston, Bill, *The Osprey Encyclopaedia of Russian Aircraft 1875-1995* (Osprey, 1995)

Jackson, A.J., *Avro Aircraft since 1908* (Putnam Aeronautical Books, 3rd edition, 2000)

Jackson, Robert, *Combat Aircraft Prototypes since 1945* (Airlife, 1985)

Moyes, Philip J.R., *Bomber Squadrons of the RAF and their Aircraft* (MacDonald, 1964)

Nemececk, Vaclav, *The History of Soviet Aircraft from 1918* (Willow Books, 1986)

Swanborough, Gordon, and Bowers, Peter M., *United States Military Aircraft since 1909* (Putnam Aeronautical Books, revised edition, 1989)

Swanborough, Gordon, and Bowers, Peter M., *United States Navy Aircraft since 1911* (Putnam Aeronautical Books, 2nd edition, 1976)

Thetford, Owen, *Aircraft of the Royal Air Force since 1918* (Putnam Aeronautical Books, 9th edition, 1995)